Handbook of

Organizational Behaviour and Human Resources

Attention Authors

Manas Publications is fighting a war to tell the world that India can win the battle not only by the bullet but also by pen. There is no dearth of intellectuals in our country, but their knowledge is confined to them only. No sincere effort has been made by any other publisher to channelise their knowledge in national interest, which is why the talent of large number of intellectuals remain latent. An author always gives the raw material in the shape of a manuscript and it is the job of the publisher to convert it into a beautiful book. Manas always motivates the intellectuals by publishing their manuscripts since more than four decades and would like to publish your manuscript too. If you or your colleagues have any manuscript ready for publication or are working on it, kindly contact us with a detailed synopsis and list of contents for its best publication. If you wish, we can also suggest you a suitable title for writing related to your area of expertise. Manas is known for its publishing quality and commitments. We take utmost care in production and give wide publicity to the book as well as its author through our national and international distribution network.

Handbook of

Organizational Behaviour and Human Resources

Swati Sharma

Manas Publications
(We Convert Fighters into Writers)
New Delhi-110002 (INDIA)

MANAS PUBLICATIONS
We Convert Fighters into Writers
(Publishers, Library Suppliers, Importers & Exporters)
4402/5-A, Ansari Road (Opp. HDFC Bank)
Darya Ganj, New Delhi-110 002 (INDIA)
Off. ✆ 23260783, 23265523, Fax: 011-23272766
E-mail: manaspublications@gmail.com
manaspublications@vsnl.com
Website: www.manaspublications.in

ISBN 978-81-7049-420-1
Rs. 495/-

Typeset at
Manas Publications

Printed in India at
Harmain Offset Press, Delhi
and published by Mrs Suman Lata for
Manas Publications, 4402/5-A, Ansari Road
(Opp. HDFC Bank),
Darya Ganj, New Delhi-110 002 (INDIA)

DEDICATED

to my Late Mother and
my Late Grandfather . . .

ACKNOWLEDGEMENTS

This is the first major writing endeavour of my life. I would like to thank some of the important people who encouraged me morally, boosted my confidence, and shared their views on the proposed content. Their contribution is invaluable in laying the foundation for this piece of writing.

Prof. Gopa Bharadwaj is the one who helped me shape up as an independent individual. The thought of writing began when Prof. Gopa asked me to write research articles under her supervision. These are the true sentiments which need to be expressed and catharsis has brought me to the world of writing.

The thought of writing a book was not shared with many of my teachers and professors but their teaching and my experiential learning has brought out a tribute to some of my guides during my journey from school to college.

I always wanted to thank them but being shy and reclusive I failed to do so. Now, from this platform I express my gratitude to them and acknowledge their contribution in my work.

My father, Mr. Ajay Sharma, and one of my close friends, Sushma, encouraged me to venture into the field of writing. I thank them for their faith in me.

I also seek blessings and reviews from the readers of this book.

– Swati Sharma

PREFACE

Human Resource (HR) and Organizational Behaviour (OB) form the backbone of any organization. The process of HR and OB operates right from the time of recruitment till the submission of resignation. In such a scenario, it has become important to understand the terminology associated with it and to check the avenues of education and careers in Human Resources/Organizational Behaviour along with understanding the remuneration packages available in the market.

This work, **Handbook of Organizational Behaviour and Human Resources,** is unique in terms of content and quality. This handbook is useful for graduates, postgraduates, managers and laymen. In India, no such handbook is available for the students which would help them understand various terms related to this field.

Further, this handbook contains the formats of HR documents. It may be helpful for the readers to understand how HR documents will look like. It shall also be useful for small and developing organizations which are in the process of structuring their HR departments.

After completion of studies in OB and HR, students are often confused about its scope. I have listed various openings that exist in the corporate and academia along with remunerations that are generally offered. However, these remuneration scales are subject to change during the process of negotiation.

I hope this work, which is one of its kind, will carve a special place amongst its readers. I wish good luck to all the readers. Please do feel free to share your opinions with me on: swati6990@yahoo.co.in.

–Swati Sharma

Contents

Section I

Processes of Organizational Behaviour and Human Resources

1

TASKS OF RECRUITMENT

DEFINITION OF RECRUITMENT

"Searching for and obtaining potential job candidates in sufficient numbers and quality so that the organization can select the most appropriate people to fill its job needs". This is how recruitment is defined by Dowling & Schuler.

Recruitment has the following objectives:

1. Projecting the positive and lucrative picture of the careers in the organization to the candidates who come searching jobs.
2. Recruiting right candidate for the right job.
3. It has an important role to play right from candidates' prejoining formalities to maintaining records of the employees during their employment before they leave by their will, or deal with cases of termination and sacking and cases of retirement.

CONCEPTUAL MEANING

The overall aim of the recruitment and selection process should be to obtain at minimum cost the number and quality of employees required to satisfy the human resources needs of the company.

It should follow three stages:

1. Defining requirements
2. Attracting candidates
3. Selecting candidates

Defining Requirements

The number and categories of people required should be specified in the requirement programme which is derived from the organization's human resource plan. Requirements for particular positions are set out in the form of job descriptions (or role definitions) and person specifications. These provide the basic information required to draft advertisements, brief recruitment agency consultants and assess candidates.

Job descriptions or role definitions describe:

- Basic details of the job
- Reporting relationships
- Overall objectives of the job
- Main activities or tasks to be carried out
- Special requirements/features (mobility, travelling or insocial hours)
- Terms and conditions of the job (pay, benefits, etc.)

Person specifications/recruitment, personnel or job specifications:

- Define education
- Define qualification
- Define training
- Describe experience requirement
- Describe competencies required by the job holder

Other specifications that may be outlined are: Meeting the candidates' expectations in terms of career opportunity, training, security, etc., the corporate culture and the need for candidates to be able to work within it.

Attracting Candidates

Attracting candidates is primarily a matter of identifying, evaluating and using the most appropriate sources of applicants. It is necessary to carry out a preliminary study of the factors that are likely to attract or repel candidates; for example, the strengths and weaknesses of the organization as an employer.

A. Analysis of recruitment strengths and weaknesses of the organization: It should cover:

- National or local reputation of the organization
- Pay
- Employee benefits
- Working conditions
- Intrinsic interest of the job
- Security of employment
- Opportunities of education and training
- Career prospects
- Location of the office or plant

The aim of the analysis of recruitment strengths and weaknesses is to prepare a better image of the organization for use in ad brochures or interviews. The analysis also shows where the organization needs to improve as an employer if it is to attract more or better candidates and to retain those selected.

For the survey use of an attitude questionnaire can be made.

B. Analysis of job features and likely sources of applicants: This analysis focuses on the following areas:

- How many jobs have to be filled in and by when?
- Refer to job descriptions and person specifications (to obtain information on responsibilities, qualifications and experience required)
- From where suitable candidates come (companies, campuses, which part of the country, etc.)
- Define the terms and conditions of the job (pay and benefits) and think whether the job or the organization would attract good candidates
- Anticipate possible objections.
- Analyse previous successes or failures (to establish what does or does not work).

C. Deciding and placing the job advertisement

Advertising agency can:

- Provide a good copy and catchy headlines.

- Devise an attractive house style and prepare layouts about the text and use of logo.
- Advise on ways of achieving visual impact by use of illustrations and special typographical features.
- Advise on media and help in response analysis.

How to choose an ad agency?

- Check its experience in handling recruitment ad.
- See examples of its work.
- Check with its clients on the level of service provided by it.
- Meet the staff who will work on the ad.
- Check the fee structure.

Choose type of ad as per your requirement

- In classified/run-on ads, copy is run on, with no white space in or around the ad and no paragraph spacing or indentation. These are cheap but suitable only for junior or routine jobs.
- In classified/semi-display ads, headings can be set in capitals, paragraphs can be indented and space is allowed around the ad. These ads are fairly cheap. A semi-display can be much more effective than a run-on advertisement.
- Full display ads are bordered and in them any type face and illustrations can be used. These ads are expensive but are most suitable for management, technical and professional jobs.

Selecting Candidates

- Main selection methods used at interview assessment centres are: psychological tests, application blanks, bio-data, interview and references. These are good sources of information about the individual candidate.
- Accuracy of selection methods such as structured interview, bio-data, personality test and assessment centres is high than typical interviews, references, graphology and astrology. Psychological tests should be used to extend the data obtained from the interview.

- If there is more than one eligible candidate for a job, it may be advisable to hold one or two people in reserve because applicants often withdraw after consenting to join.

2

Types and Sources of Employee

The optimum level of employees for each department is prepared by the HR department in consultation with the department head and after obtaining approval from the GM. Then the proposed employee strength is sanctioned by the vice president (operations)/president.

The employee strength for each department will be reviewed once a year by the manager (Human Resources) with the concerned department heads. Proposals for increase or decrease in the employee strength or change of designation or creation of new positions or any other changes affecting levels and types of employees in the company must have the approval of the general manager, vice president (operations) and president. For the purpose of analyzing the actual employee strength of a unit, the following categories of employees would be taken into consideration.

- **Permanent:** A permanent employee is a person who has been engaged on a regular basis and has been confirmed in writing as a permanent employee either at the time of initial recruitment or after satisfactory completion of the stipulated probationary period applicable to him/her as per his/her employment terms in the same or any other occupation in the organization. An employee would not be deemed to be permanent unless confirmed in writing.
- **Probationary:** A probationer is a person who is provisionally employed to fill a regular vacancy in a

post and has not completed the stipulated probationary period applicable to his/her grade. On satisfactory completion of the probationary period, the probationer's service will be confirmed in writing. If the probationary period is not completed satisfactorily, then either the probationary period may be suitably extended or his/her services may be terminated. Termination will apply also to the extended period of probation.

- **Trainee:** A trainee is a person engaged for imparting in-house training in specific trades or occupations under a training agreement. Trainees do not have an employer-employee relationship. They are hired for the explicit purpose of imparting training as per the training agreement signed.
- **Apprentice:** An apprentice is a person who is undergoing apprenticeship training in pursuance of a contract of apprenticeship or educational curriculum.
- **Temporary:** A temporary is a person who has been temporarily engaged for work which is essentially of permanent nature likely to be determined within a limited span of period. In case the department head feels that the performance of the temporary employee is good and wishes to retain him/her on his/her completion of the six-month period, the temporary employee would be subjected to regular interview. And, if found suitable, the termporary employee may be engaged as a regular trainee under a training agreement. And, if not found suitable, the services of the temporary employee must be discontinued immediately. This category of employees may be engaged in any department as per the requirement.
- **Contractual employee:** A contractual employee is one whose contract of employment is for a specific period and stands terminated automatically as stipulated in the contract if the contract is not renewed.

The following categories constitute the buffer strength:

- **Casual/daily wager:** A casual is a person whose employment is of casual nature. He works on hourly or daily rate basis.

- **Leave vacancy employees:** A leave vacancy employee is a person who is engaged in place of a permanent employee or probationer who is temporarily absent. This engagement is only for the period the concerned permanent employee or probationer is on leave without pay or maternity leave and will cease automatically on his/her rejoining duty.

SOURCES OF RECRUITMENT

Sources of recruitment are both external and internal.

Internal Sources

Opportunities are given to existing employees who have proved their worth in other functions. For this purpose, the HR department will make known the positions that are vacant in the company on a monthly basis by notifying in the general notice board so as to invite applications from interested employees.

External Sources

- Management institutes: Administrative jobs
- Catering colleges: Skilled jobs in operations
- Secretarial schools : Secretarial jobs
- Polytechnics/ITIs: Technical jobs
- Employee exchanges
- Databank of HR department
- Placement agencies as approved by GM/manager HR
- Advertisement as per standard approved format with job specification
- Direct/walk-in applicants

Recruitment of close relatives: Recruitment of close relatives of any past or present employee of the organization and re-employment of any ex-employee of the group shall require the approval of the president.

Interview Call

Interview call letters to prospective candidates are to be sent. Travelling and conveyance for the interview is not normally reimbursed as a matter of policy. However, in case of outstation candidates prior permission of the GM/vice president (operations) is taken for conveyance reimbursement.

The applications of the rejected candidates along with comments of the interviews should be kept categorized position within the HR department for a period of 3 years for the managerial level applications and ½ year for the rest of applications.

Pre-employment Requirements

The manager HR must ensure that the following documents have been collected from the candidate and formalities completed.

1. Prior to final interview

HR receives the following documents from the candidate:

- Employment application form and coloured stamp size photograph
- Birth certificate/proof of age
- Qualification certificates
- Experience certificate from previous employers
- Police clearance

2. Prior to Joining

(a) HR issues offer letter

(b) HR receives from the candidate three copies of coloured, stamp size photograph which should be used for the following purposes:

- Identity card
- Identity-cum-magnetic time card
- Security identification register
- Temporary identification card
- Copy of resignation letter

(c) HR gets completed the following formalities:

- ESI declaration form, wherever applicable
- PF nomination form
- Issue welcome letter enclosing the grooming ticket

3. On Joining

Issue the magnetic time card, locker, keys, update the security identification register, issue of appointment letter with job description and tip policy, issue of employee handbook, induction kit, completion of bank account formalities by the employee and uniform formalities.

4. Pre-employment medical examination:

It is essential for all employees to have a medical test before joining the services of the organization. Pathological tests need to be conducted in accordance with the medical test reference slip in a pathological laboratory designated by the organization. On receipt of the medical test reports, a thorough examination of the candidate must be conducted and a pre-employment medical test form must be filled out by the organization's designated doctor. If the doctor finds that the candidate is in need of any treatment, he will prescribe the same, which the candidate will have to take at his/her own expense. The candidate will be re-examined by the doctor to be declared fit. If the doctor finds the candidate absolutely unfit for employment, the candidate will stand rejected.

3

Role of Resume, References, IIS in Recruitment

Atul is trying hard to get noticed in the job market. And there are several others like Atul who are working hard to cling to any opportunity that offers them space for work. This is one aspect of truth. There is other side of truth as well. One posting of sales representative created in Ahmedabad or any other metropolitan city drew a response of 450 resumes over the first weekend. In another instance, my good friend John sent his resume to a company and soon learned that he was one of 700 candidates. Though very capable, John didn't get the job.

HOW TO STAND APART FROM THE CROWD?

Among major factors which can make or mar you chance of getting a job is your resume. Your resume is more than what is printed on 8½ by 11 inch sheet of paper. It communicates valuable information to hiring managers. It expresses who you are, and what you do or did best. It tells the reader how you can add value to the organization. One should be creative to stand apart from the crowd. But don't forget protocol. So, you need to ask yourself this all important question: What can I do to make my resume stand out?

One should be aware of the following points while preparing one's resume:

- The basic format and style of your resume.
- Mention of the different job titles you've had that

may or may not represent skills transferable to the job you are applying for.

- About education, where and what you studied, what level you achieved, whether you received any recognition or honours.
- For the length of the resume, the rule of thumb is: resumes should rarely be more than two pages. In most industries less is more
- The basic aesthetics and feel of the resume: fonts, blank spaces, and choice of paper — reflect who you are. And neatness counts.

In other words, bio-data covers a wide variety of information about individuals and their background including age, sex, place of birth, place of residence, family background, number of brothers and sisters, education, work experience, marital status, number of children, physical characteristics (such as height and weight), medical history, hobbies, reading habits, etc. Building a personal portfolio entails maintaining a written record of skills, accomplishments, knowledge, aptitudes and lessons learned at each job. Such a portfolio is useful for self-assessment, marketing and storing up-to-date information. The personal portfolio helps individuals take inventory of what skills they have, how their skills add value to the organization and how their skills can be repackaged for new job opportunities. The personal portfolio can also be useful in determining what knowledge and experiences necessary for today workplace are absent so that action plans can be formed to obtain them.

WHAT'S IMPORTANT FOR THE EMPLOYER?

Let's see why resume is important and what feature of resume attracts industry people?

Resume expresses the key areas which are reflected in knowledge and experience, career objective and hobbies. Career objective is very important as it shows what the person thinks, and the hobbies reflect his/her personality. A fine talk of 5 minutes will reveal the personality of the candidate, and whether the resume is a copied one or not.

In other words, key areas of the resume clearly define the job profile of the candidate.

One HR expert terms the resume as the first and the last impression. Resume gives an overview of the candidate and whether the resume matches with the job requirement or not. The features of resume which attract most of the companies are: educational qualification and experience followed by personal details. Personal details include strengths, weaknesses and hobbies. It helps in knowing how the person is going to manage in office.

Most of the companies do not check references mentioned in the resume. They think an interview by an experienced person is enough to decide whether the candidate possesses qualities required for the job.

One psychology scholar gives importance to qualification, age and address in the resume in that order to judge a candidate's competence. And, then comes the importance of the candidate's photo. The sobre presentation style and neatness of resume also go in the candidate's favour. So remember, a concise writing style, correct spelling and visually appealing presentation of different details in your resume give you an edge over your competitors.

GETTING DOWN TO WRITING

A resume sends a cultural message to interviewers. There are a billion ways to create one. Let's see how to write one:

1. Your name should be in a bold font larger than the rest. You should give the complete address including your landline, mobile, and office phone numbers. Give as many numbers as possible because when recruiters call, they would prefer to reach you immediately. Email address is also essential as one would want to document the interview call because your current salary, expected salary, job profile details can be shared better via the email than on phone.
2. Write a summary of what you want to do or a short description of what you have been trained to do.

3. List your work experience. This is the part that everyone looks at carefully: where you have worked, what you have done and what you accomplished while doing it. This should include:
   - Company name, state and position held
   - Education
   - Special training certifications
4. References are important as they confirm your aptitude, attributes and achievements. They are for verification of your qualifications. The list of references can include past supervisors, peers, customers, vendors and people who have known you for a long time. You should print your reference list on an 8½ by 11 inch piece of paper. It should include:
   - Name of contact
   - Company contacts
   - Relationship with the candidate
   - Referee's address along with phone numbers
5. *Vote of thanks*: A thank you note may not seem like a big deal, but it really is! You should express thanks to the person (the recruiter) who has gone through your resume as he/she has invested both time and energy on you.

TYPES OF RESUME

Now let's know about three basic types of resume.

A. Chronological Resume

Format

- Objective
- Experience
- Education

It highlights:

- Track record of your achievements.
- Job title and tenure in the job.
- Growth in experience and responsibility.
- What you have done and accomplished.

B. Functional Resume

Format

- Profile description
- Skills listing
- Experience
- Education

It highlights:

- Points that are relevant to the entry-level job. (This resume type is useful when you have no or little work experience.)
- Qualifications that might not be visible from a list of past titles or positions.

C. Combination Resume

Format

- Profile description
- Experience — skills
- Education

It highlights:

- Your transferable skills, achievements, and qualifications in one document.
- A strong connection between your work experience and areas of responsibility. This helps the recruiter see how your skill could be used in another situation.
- Common strengths and abilities when your experience doesn't show a clear-cut career direction.

PRESENTATION/WRITING

Before you adopt any style for writing your resume, you should remember the following points:

- The career objective is in line with the position advertised.
- The body of resume supports the objective.
- The resume should showcase all the possible answers to the most important questions that the interviewer will ask.

- The most important elements of your work experience should appear on the top half of the first page.
- Your resume, especially your achievements, should begin with action verbs. They should be quantified when needed.
- Use present tense when talking about your current job and past tense when referring to your past job.
- It's easy to read the text divided in points separated by lots of white space.
- Ensure that someone else has proofread the resume for grammar and checked the types of fonts used.
- Use key words appropriate for the industry or the potential employer.
- Writing a cover letter to hiring managers is part of the application process in some cases. The cover letter should include an introduction about yourself, an explanation of why you are contacting the manager, a brief summary of the talents you possess and how they may align with the vacant position and a personalized message to the company you are sending it to.

APPLICATION BLANKS

The amount of required information varies from small details about name, age, address, phone number, etc. to a ten-page document covering all aspects of previous education, work history, and private life.

Application blanks generally have two functions:

1. They provide information about individuals needed by the organizations which hire them. For example, age, sex, number of dependants, social security, etc.
2. They are designed to gather such information about job applicants that the HR officer feels is important to the hiring process.

Application blanks may lead to selection even before interview and hence may lead to biases.

REFERENCES

References are documents which provide information about the candidate's technical and soft skills. Soft skills include communication, team building, leadership qualities and much more. References are based upon referee's observation about the candidate over a good period of time. The referee should be skilled and a good observer. He/she should give genuine feedback about candidate's ability to perform and his/her attitude towards life. For this purpose references are required in organizations.

Personal referees are useless. All they prove is that the applicant has at least one or two friends. Written references are standard. They save time and help in commenting on the applicant's character in general and confirming his employment record.

Opinions on reference checking vary in the industry. Some people in the corporate world believe that reference checking is not reliable though some others consider it a must for any kind of recruitment activity. There are two limitations about references. First, the candidates will provide only such references that will give positive information about them. Second, only the references provided by the candidates could be checked. It should be understood that references can be obtained from peers and colleagues rather than depending upon the immediate boss or any boss in that particular vertical where the candidate belongs.

While talking to references one should listen carefully and make notes about long pauses, number of pauses, silence observed, hesitations and deliberate choice of wording. It is desirable that reference checking should be based on open-ended questions rather than close-ended questions. For example, "In what way John could be useful for us?" Close-ended questions give respondents too much time to think and therefore only an abstract of the information can be obtained. These questions should be based upon the Interview Imaging Scorecard or IIS. IIS is explained in the next topic. The following questions about an employee, say John, may be put to his references:

- What are the traits that attracted you while you planned to replace John?
- If he was doing well, what was the need to look for another candidate?

- What was the reaction of employees towards John on work?
- In what areas John was showing a malfunctioning status?
- In what way John brought laurels to the job?

While checking a reference, there is a legal aspect as well. First, it should be true and provided to only those who need them. It should be precise and limited to the requirements of the job. It should not be directed to ruin the candidate's reputation. It is a do-it-yourself job. Peers can be helpful. Verify the identity of the referee. It should be done by phone or face-to-face because in writing it will show only the dates of employment and termination. Asking somebody to give a reference is asking a favour. Questions should be planned before. Be brief and candid. Information should be held confidential and to be used by only the recruitment staff and other specialists of the job. The people who are posing as referees should stick to the facts rather than personal judgement arising out of the halo effect.

INTERVIEW IMAGING SCORE CARD (IIS)

There is a difficult question — Whether we can have a perfect candidate that can be found out by a perfect selection procedure? It remains unanswered! There is no perfect format through which we can have an effective, objective evaluation process. A certain amount of subjectivity does always creep in.

Let's have the format which is displayed below:

Candidate	Parameter 1 Experience	Parameter 2 Qualification	Parameter 3 Appearance	Total
Rohit	2	1	5	8
Seema	3	4	2	9
Atul	5	5	4	14

Scoring Key

A candidate can be assessed on a 5-point scale — 1 stands for very poor, 2 stands for poor, 3 stands for average, 4 stands for good, and 5 stands for very good. The highest score is 5 and the lowest score is 1. These scores help you decide which candidate should be hired.

The IIS card helps the interviewer focus on desired specific parameter on the 5-point scale. The scores are added row-wise to get a total score. Assessment can be made on two scores which emerge after the process of scoring — (1) Row-wise total score can be compared among different candidates. (2) Each parameter can have intra- and inter-comparisons, i.e. the interviewer can see on which parameter a particular candidate scores high and also how different candidates have scored on a particular dimension/parameter.

Sometimes the candidate with a low score is selected as at times the company needs low-profile candidates who can be trained according to the organization's culture. After all, interviewers have their own biases. It is important to ensure that the interviewer has complete knowledge about the dimensions/parameters that are formulated to assess the candidate. Evaluating a candidate on the basis of experience depends on the organizaion's expectations from the candidate — Whether it wants a candidate who requires no training and is ready to embark on this new job? Or, it requires a candidate who needs some amount of supervision. And, the third type would be the candidate who is creative and has the ability to step out of his/her shoes.

The interviewer can have any number of dimensions, from 5 to 8. It is so because minimum number of dimensions offers a comprehensive assessment. Which dimensions should be given prominence depends on the discretion of the interviewer. Questions should be framed according to the chosen dimensions. These questions should be preferably 10, and the interview time limit should be 40 to 60 minutes. After 40 minutes, the interviewer should be able to decide— Should the candidate be hired or not? And further, if the candidate is to be brought into the organization, what will the organization gain and lose from the strengths and weaknesses of the candidate.

Questions can be based the following sources of information about the candidate.

- The candidate's resume provides preliminary information.
- Some initial information such as communication skill and the ability to carry oneself is also obtained from the initial round of interview.

- The candidate's tenure of experience helps the interviewer decide what questions should be asked from a list of 25 to 30 questions. Ten important questions may be asked.

The candidate's answers to some questions may reflect his/her tendency to change the job when faced with a difficult situation. Here is an example. It is shown below:

Manager: When you realized you might fail into maths, what did you do?

Candidate: I changed my stream.

On the IIS, it is important for the interviewer to test whether the candidate's interest lies in what he/she has chosen. The interviewer should keep in mind that he/she is not hiring a sailing enthusiast but an accountant or system analyst. When people are interested in what they do, they make efforts to get better at it.

Here are some questions to zero is on the candidate's real interests:

- What ways you have incorporated in order to become effective in your job domain?
- What provides you satisfaction?
- When, how and why did you make an extra effort in your job domain?
- What situations in your personal and professional spheres made you learn something novel?
- What are your goals? And why you want to achieve only those goals?

Don't ask, "What do you plan for the next five years?" Instead, shape your probe in the following way:

- What are your expectations while working in this organization which you have failed to fulfil in your present or previous organizations?
- What pulls you towards this job description?
- What is the most significant aspect that you are searching for?

The candidate who comes to your company is certainly looking for that aspect which is absent in his previous or present organizations. Had this candidate been satisfied with his job he would not have come for the interview.

During the last few minutes, the interviewer should ask about the candidate's spare-time activities. If the candidate says that "I am interested in boating, weightlifting and bungee jumping", it indicates that activities other than work excite this person. And, eventually one can lead to this interpretation that this candidate is not psychologically indulged in the work even in instances where he/she has shown significant success.

Note Taking and Scoring the Sheet

Before starting the interview, three sheets would be taken care of — candidate's bio-data or resume, 4-6" sheet for note taking and another sheet carrying 25-30 questions. IIS should be inside the desk so that the candidate does not get to see it.

It is advisable to the interviewers to take notes. This will help in recollecting what happened during the interview time. A 4-6" paper should be used so that you will not be taking notes extensively. Further, it should be conveyed to the interviewee that some note taking activity will be followed up during the interview. It is better to put down a key word rather than noting down everything what the candidate is saying. Key words will help you remember the entire conversation with greater clarity. Use of key words will also help you prevent consecutive breaking up of the eye contact with the candidate.

Do the scoring as soon as possible after the interview finishes. When you intend to involve other experts for the decision, divide up the IIS sheet. By doing this, the candidate will get different sets of questions by different interviewers.

Benefits of using the IIS sheet are:

1. More appropriate fixers
2. Use of silence
3. More effective recall
4. More competent interviewing

5. Involves different experts effectively
6. Focus on the job description
7. Reduces personal biases and subjectivity

The IIS strategy forces the interviewer to analyze the job before analyzing the candidate for the job. This strategy, however, is not immune to the impact of these factors, i.e. mood of the interviewer, the number of interviews conducted in a day, the time or day of the interview and the quality of the previous candidate. The mood of the interviewer will affect the process though use of the IIS reduces this subjectivity to some extent. It will affect in evaluating the candidate and patient listening to the answers of the candidate. If the interviewer has been taking interviews throughout the day, he/she can be tiresome and this may impact his/her markings. The time of lunch or the time when the office closes may end the interview haphazardly. The quality of the previous candidate may lead to the contrast error. The interviewer may evaluate the candidate by comparing with the previous candidates before putting the markings on the IIS sheet.

It helps in practicing to listen and evaluate at the same time. Silence offers space for the interviewee to put his/her views easily. Use of IIS makes the interviewer phrase questions related to the dimensions stated on the IIS sheet. This prevents the interviewer to indulge in trying to devise another question which he/she will put forward as soon as the candidate finishes.

The IIS strategy helps to recall everything about each candidate as note taking is part of the strategy.

The IIS strategy prevents you from hiring a candidate out of halo effect. If a candidate says he is good in metaphysics, reading the aura of each person through photograph, name or phone voice then your response may be: "Fantastic". And, you end up hiring the candidate. Now if we objectively question it, nowhere in the job description it is mentioned that metaphysics is needed to perform the job. And, the selected candidate comes to you after five months saying that you don't use his metaphysical competence. He ends up leaving the job. In such a scenario, the entire interviewing procedure turns into a flop.

Use of different experts helps bring variety of questions, and the onus of failure or success of the interview lies equally on the people who are on the expert panel.

The IIS strategy helps the interviewer look objectively at the candidate's knowledge, skills and abilities and evaluate the pay package against the particular requirements of a particular job position.

The IIS strategy is more objective because each candidate is compared to the same list of requirements.

4

ROLE OF PSYCHOMETRIC TESTING IN MANAGEMENT PRACTICE

Psychometrics is the field of study concerned with the educational and psychological measurement. It includes the measurement of knowledge, abilities, and personality traits of different of persons. The measurement instruments used in this study are questionnaires and tests.

Psychometric or psychological tests have found a profound place in the area of management. They are no more confined to clinical practice or social set-up. These are used up by numerous companies and authorities worldwide to select and recruit staff at all levels — from entry level to CEO. These tests figure prominently in the staff selection procedures of police, civil service, local authorities, armed forces, health services, financial institutions, retail sector companies, motor industry, IT industry, management consultants, airlines, power industry, etc. In recent times, its usage has increased in India but it is already used widely in Europe, Australia and the USA.

WHAT IS A PSYCHOMETRIC TEST?

Psychometric tests are structured tests, taken in exam-like conditions, which aim to measure objectively a person's ability or certain aspects of his/her personality. They are devised by occupational psychologists. Their aim is to provide employers with a reliable method of selecting suitable applicants. These tests are designed carefully so that they are fair to all applicants. Let us understand the conceptual meaning of a psychometric or psychological test. According to Murphy and Shofer, the psychological test is a measurement instrument that has three defining characteristics:

- It is a sample of behaviour.
- The sample is obtained under standardized conditions.
- There are established rules for scoring to obtain quantitative information from the sample of behaviour.

According to Freeman, "A psychological test is a standardized instrument designed to measure objectively one or more aspects of a total personality by means of a sample of verbal or non-verbal responses or by means of other behaviour."

According to Anastasi, "A psychological test is essentially an objective and standardized measure of a sample of behaviour."

The roots of psychological testing can be traced back to ancient times. Over 3000 years ago, the Chinese used written tests for filling civil service posts. At the turn of the eighteenth century the following pioneers made important contribution to the field of psyhological testing. Francis Galton stimulated investigations of individual differences and also directed his experimental efforts to measure intelligence by means of tests of imagery and sensory discrimination. He devised a test for the measurement of the delicacy of weight discrimination. In 1905 Binet devised a test to measure differences in mental development — in degree of brightness or dullness with difference in the level of development. He gave impetus to the study of individual differences by means of standardized tests. The great development in testing and studying individual differences in the United States occurred after Binet's work was made known. James McKeen Cattell, a young contemporary of Galton, first employed the term "mental tests". Cattell's tests were of memory, imagery, keenness of eye sight, colour preferences and reaction time.

NOT A MEASURE OF PERSONALITY ONLY

A common misconception is that psychometric tests only measure personality which is not the case as there are a variety of tests which measure your different abilities. Some measure your ability to understand the written word or to reason with numbers. Others measure your ability to solve mechanical problems or follow instructions accurately or understand data which is presented in a variety of ways. There are the personality tests, assessing everything from motivation to working preferences. But psychometric tests cannot measure everything. For example they cannot measure enthusiasm.

Broadly, psychological tests are classified into areas like aptitude tests, personality inventories, interest inventories, tests of motivation and attitude, projective tests, organizational climate survey, organizational culture survey, employee satisfaction/engagement survey, and intelligence quotient tests.

CHARACTERISTICS OF A PSYCHOLOGICAL TEST

- A psychological test is a sample of behaviour. In other words, a psychological test attempts to approximate the exhaustive procedure of measuring all the possible behaviours used in measuring a particular attribute by collecting a systematic sample of behaviour. Secondly, such behaviour sample measures psychological variables in such a way that the quality of a test is largely determined by the representations of this sample. For example, to develop a test for writing ability would not mean to collect and evaluate everything that a person has written from term papers to laundry lists. This is impractical and also it does not ensure the quality of a test. To ensure practicality and representativeness of the behaviour, the test should include a series of short essays, sample letters, memos, etc., which make the test more meaningful.
- The sample is obtained under standardized conditions and is also scored and interpreted under standardized procedures. Let us understand the standardized administration of the test through the following example: A scholastic aptitude test is administered to thousands of students. Here, a test supervisor reads detailed instructions to all examinees before starting, and each portion of the test is timed. The test manual includes exhaustive instructions dealing with appropriate seating

patterns, lighting, interruptions and emergencies. Standardized scoring procedure includes same set of scoring rules applied to many people taking the same test. Standardized interpretation of the test score includes the way test scores are interpreted. All this minimizes the role of the examiner.

- Psychological tests are designed to measure specific attributes of a person, not the whole person.
- They only tell us ways in which individuals are similar or different.
- Psychological tests are invariably imperfect, i.e. they may not provide an adequate measure of a specific attribute of two people. For example, John may receive a high score than Mary on a test of spatial ability. But in reality, he may have the ability equal to that of Mary.
- Psychological tests are reliable to some extent as they do provide an adequate measure of a particular attribute and assign scores in a consistent fashion.
- These tests are used to make inferences about people. There are two types of inferences which one might make on the basis of test scores. First, the inferences regarding the attribute being measured. Second, the inferences regarding the decisions about individuals. These inferences are called validity of measurement and validity of decisions.
- Psychological tests assume significance because they are scored on the basis of standardized norms. A norm-based score indicates where an individual stands in comparison to a particular normative group that defines the set of standards. The norms are empirically established by determining what a representative group of persons actually does on the test. Psychological test norms are in no sense absolute, universal or permanent. They merely represent the test performance of the persons constituting standardized sample.

These days many employers are so particular about psychometric tests that they put them on their application forms and websites. These tests could also pop up later in their process, or even after you've been offered the job when your new boss is deciding exactly where in the organization to place you. In theory, all psychometric tests given to job applicants should be relevant to the job. However, many organizations use verbal, numerical and abstract reasoning tests as a matter of routine, no matter what the job description says. So be prepared to take more than one test. In India, the human resource department takes care of getting these tests administered.

Most psychometric tests are paper and pencil tests, but a growing number of tests have now been designed to be taken sitting at a computer. Computerized testing is becoming increasingly common. The format is always that of a multiple choice questionnaire. The questions appear on the screen, and you click your answer choices with the mouse. Within a few seconds of finishing the test, your score is emailed to the examiner.

If you take a test at home, you don't need to worry about getting anywhere on time , you don't have to take a day off and you don't even need to get dressed. Plus, you should find out if the organization is interested in taking your application any further within a few minutes, which is a million times better than waiting for them to send you a letter. The only thing you need to do when taking a test on your home computer is make sure the person taking the test is you!

Tips for a Good Psychometric Score

- Sleep well during the night.
- If you have any impairment or are physically challenged then let your tester know this.
- Give responses that describe you the best.
- Attempt all the questions.
- Let your first response be your final response.
- If you wear spectacles or use a hearing aid and then do carry them along.
- Don't skip your meal because feeling hungry might hamper your concentration during the test.
- Stay calm and composed.

- Read the instructions properly or ask your tester.
- Do practise the examples before you proceed for the test.
- Normally these tests don't require any preparation, but for numerical test you can practise on formulae and some examples.

Psychometric tests can be used to challenge stereotype judgements by interviewers and often enable a more objective analysis to take place while interviewing alone or in a group. Psychometric tests should be used only by qualified professionals such as psychologists. These tests can turn out to be potentially dangerous if they fall into the wrong hands. When properly administered, these tests help ensure a common language for assessment and interpretation throughout the organization. It is very vital that there is a match between skills and characteristics measured with the job or organizational demands. However, to institutionalize the use of psychometric tests in the company, the cost is high because a separate department of at least 1-2 persons is required additionally to carry out this task.

5

What is an Interview?

The interview schedule is a tool of social sciences. It involves a set of questions related to social, political and cognitive issues. It is a tool to get information from the respondent concerning various psychological and sociological issues. Interview means "conversation with a purpose" (Bingham & Moore, 1941).

Data which could be attained from elsewhere are part of the interview record (e.g. test scores, biographical information, letters of recommendation, etc.). They give this process an edge over other selection devices. Data which are unique to the interview process are personal dress and general mannerism.

Many studies reflect the importance of interview. One of them is quoted below:

Spriegel & James (1958) examined the data from a 1930 survey of 236 firms and a 1957 survey of 852 firms. In the 1930 survey, 93% of the firms reported using interview as part of their selection process. By 1957 their number increased to 99%.

FEATURES/OBJECTIVES OF INTERVIEW

Interviews used in the industry differ according to their objectives. Some important objectives of interview are:

- It may be used as an exploratory device to identify variables and study hypothesis.
- It is used as a supplementary device to validate other methods, e.g. the questionnaire method.

- It is used as a main instrument for studying relationships among various variables and hypothesis.
- Candidates are evaluated through interview for purposes of hiring, promotion or transfer. Such interviews are referred to as selection or placement interviews.
- Interview is used to obtain information concerning the employee's attitude about his/her job, the company, etc. These interviews are referred to as attitude interviews.
- Many interviews are carried out during employment or at the point of termination. Such interviews are called exit or separation interviews.
- Interview is used to provide on-the-job help. Such interviews are called counselling interviews.
- Interview is used to evaluate the employee under difficult situation. Such interviews are called assessment or stress interviews.

Despite the above stated objectives, interview often is difficult to evaluate as a selection device because the purpose of the interview is:

- To gather as much data relevant to the selection.
- To evaluate the data available and decide whether to select or reject the applicant.
- Type of interviews
- Degree of training which the interviewer has received
- His biases
- The position he is directed to fill
- Duration of the interview
- Type of interviews

FACTORS AFFECTING INTERVIEW

Symonds (1939) has listed a series of factors which he believes can influence the quality and quantity of the data collected during interview.

1. **Factors inherent in the applicant:** Age, intelligence, sex, race, socio-economic level,

language ability, emotional quotient, security, applicant's attitude toward interviewer, applicant's previous acquaintance with the interview process and his/her purpose of coming to the interview.

2. **Factors inherent in the interviewer:** Age, sex, intelligence, race, socio-economic level, position with reference to the applicant, personality (sociability, sympathy, empathy, human interest and credibility), social outlook, psychological understanding (ability to sense or feel the purposes, needs or drives of the applicant), previous acquaintance, interest of the interviewer in the applicant (degree to which the interviewer enjoys conversation with the interviewee).
3. **Situational factors:** Factors such as place, time, person's present, first, second or immediately preceding interview experience, emergency character of the interview, directions given to the applicant preceding the interview and voluntary versus non-voluntary nature of the interview.
4. **Factors in the form and content of interview:** Content of questions, form of questions, interpretation, suggestion or other reactions of the interviewer, purpose of the interview, identity of the interviewer, encouragement given by the interviewer, remarks interpolated by the examiner during the interview.

INTERVIEW SCHEDULE

The interview or interview schedule is classified as:

(a) **Structured interview:** In this type of interview, the list of questions is already prepared, and the questions are asked in the order they are listed. Structured interviews are also referred to as patterned interviews.

(b) **Unstructured interview:** In this type of interview, the list of questions may be there, but questions are not asked sequentially. The interviewer is free to ask in any order.

In both these types, the interview schedule has three kinds of information:

1. **Identification data:** Face, name, status, region, political, etc.
2. **Sociological variables:** Income, status, region and political affiliation, occupation level, education level, etc.
3. **Problem information:** Information concerning the main problem which is to be studied.

The items used to get information on sociological and psychological variables are of three kinds. These are:

- Fixed alternative
- Open-end questions
- Scale item

1. **Fixed alternative:** These questions are framed in such a way that the answer options for the respondent are fixed.

   Advantage: Information can be easily coded. There is uniformity of measurement, that is, everybody responds in the same order and same category.

   Limitations: Information obtained may be very superficial. Respondents may get irritated because they are interested in giving more information than responding into yes or no. Further, individuals may not respond in a sincere manner.

2. **Open-end questions:** The respondent is free to give any answer to these questions in 3 or 4 statements or a paragraph.

   Advantage: The interviewer gets information pertaining to personal issues. The pattern is quite flexible, that is, questions can be adjusted according to the respondent and the study of subject. The interviewer puts a minimum restrain on the respondent in answering because there are no fixed categories. There is possibility of in-depth answers and the investigator can study the issue in detail. Further, while probing one can clear up the misunderstanding. The interviewer can detect respondent's lack of knowledge. Open-end questions can be used to detect ambiguity. It also encourages cooperation.

Limitations: It is time consuming as the job of the interviewer is to first code the information and then tabulate it. It is not economical. It is expensive as a lot of energy and time is invested in it. Further, there is no uniformity of responses.

3. **Scale item:** Scaling of answers is somewhat like this: agree, somewhat agree, seldom agree and never agree. Such a scaling procedure is used mostly in attitude scale.

   Advantage: There is uniformity of responses. The only difference is that there are more categories. Information can be easily coded.

   Limitation: Too much analytic approach is required.

Question writing is a skill and demand experience. Criteria for question writing as proposed by Kerlinger cover the following points:

- Is the question related to the research problem?
- Is the type of question right? That is, whether scale or open-ended will be suitable. It depends upon the issue studied.
- Is the language unambiguous, i.e. is it precise and clear?
- Is the question leading? In leading questions the respondent gives an obvious answer. For example, "Do you read newspaper?" Such questions should be avoided.
- Does the question demand knowledge? Such questions should also be avoided because sometimes the respondent lacks certain level of knowledge. In such cases, first give a para to assess whether the person has certain level of information.
- Does the question demand personal information regarding open issues such as marriage? Such questions should be avoided.
- Is the question loaded with social desirability? Such questions should be avoided. For example, "Do you like to help?"

EVALUATION OF INTERVIEW AND INTERVIEW SCHEDULE

In terms of reliability and validity, we have to consider a lot many factors. These are: training of interviewers, type of question written (should be precise and simple), lack of sharp and constant focus on problem and hypothesis, lack of appreciation of schedule as a measurement instrument, lack of necessary background and experience. It should be objective about how attitude changes and develops, knowledge about persuasion and sensitive towards issues. Further, it has great potential in yielding data. Any kind of problem can be studied through interview method. Body language, facial expressions and way of responding can be noted. It is adaptable. It is suitable to all kinds of respondents. One limitation it has is that it is expensive. Despite its limitations, both as a selection technique and as a tool for research purposes, it is suitable to any kind of issue and respondent. Interview can be conducted alone or by two interviewers. Both interviewers could examine each candidate together working as a team. Each interviewer could examine each candidate separately and then hire or reject after the agreement of the other interviewer.

Don'ts for the Interviewer

Failure to establish rapport with the candidate: Rapport does not mean making friends with the candidate. Neither is it about playing psychologist to the candidate's anxieties.

Not knowing exactly what abilities are required: Not working from a meticulously developed list of requirement. Relying upon job descriptions will not be a sufficient way when the interviewer also needs to know what abilities and soft skills are required for a particular job and specific position which the candidate may hold in the hierarchy of organization.

Becoming a victim of the halo effect: Halo effect may arise when the interviewer finds something in common with the interviewee such as hailing from same college, state or even religion.

Doing most of the talking: If the interviewer fails to listen then he/she is missing the entirely important and meaningful information from the candidate. This can happen when the interviewer talks too much and listens less.

Not allowing silences to occur: The only way the interviewer can influence a reluctant candidate to speak is by keeping silent with body language.

Using too many direct questions: Direct questions generally elicit answers in yes/no. These questions can prevent the candidate from speaking smoothly and freely.

Asking questions that serve no purpose: It means the interviewer asks irrelevant questions just to fill up the time. And, this gives a hint to the candidate that the interviewer is engaged in question generation rather than listening to them.

Poor sequencing of questions: If the interview is not planned then the interviewer will jump around from one domain to other domain.

Making impulsive conclusions and generalizations based on some assumed characteristic: It may happen when the interviewer bases his judgement on the physical appearance, diction and values.

Repeating the information on the application or resume: It wastes the time but it is an excellent way to interview the candidate when one is not prepared to do so.

Selling the organization too soon: It means that the interviewer is telling the candidate about the challenging position, rewarding , advantageous, and exciting will not make it attractive to the candidate no matter how enthusiastically the interviewer imparts the information.

Ignoring intuition (gut feeling): These are the feelings which result from facts, observation (candidate's body language) and experience coming together on a subconscious level. Intuition is a sign which needs more definitive information.

Asking questions that don't give worthwhile information: This category includes (1) questions that telegraph the desired responses (listening skills), (2) apparent choices where there are none (e.g. "Do you get emotional and overreact?" Or, "Can you keep a cool head?") and questions where the answers, although obvious, cannot be checked for truthfulness.

Asking "magic questions": These questions are penetrative in nature about the candidate's personality, e.g. "If you could be an animal, which one would you choose?"

Not being knowledgeable about the legal restrictions regarding interviewing: The interviewer is expected to have a desired level of knowledge about legal matters. If the interviewer is unclear about what can and cannot be asked, he or she may fail to do a thorough interview out of fear of delving into an illegal topic.

Giving evaluative feedback/exchanging opinions with the candidate: The interview situation is not a social event and the candidate's opinions are not a concern here. So, it is not appropriate on the part of the interviewer to exchange opinions with the interviewee.

Asking multiple choice (laundry list) questions: Such pattern of questions will give an opportunity to the candidate to escape the task of thinking by simply selecting a response from the list of choices provided by the interviewer.

Excessive note taking: Taking notes in bulk will confuse the interviewer. Moreover, he/she will fail to take notice of the candidate's body language, facial expressions, tone and other miscellaneous gestures.

Giving commitments/making promises: Unintentional comments such as "I think you will be hired" will be treated as hiring commitments. And if the candidate is not hired, then the candidate may claim that he/she was guaranteed employment.

STRUCTURING THOSE 40 MINUTES

As an astute interviewer, you will need only a well thought out IIS , 10 good questions, and 40 minutes to conduct an effective interview.

Suppose you were the executive VP of a major MNC and needed a secretary. Let's say this is the 5th secretary to be placed in this position in the past 18 months. You claim that the last 5 secretaries were deficient skill-wise.

Once you have planned out how you intend to structure the 40-minute interview, you should tell the candidate what that plan is so that he/she is fully prepared to participate in the exercise. This can be done with a simple structuring statement. For example, "In this company, we make every effort to match people with jobs that draw on their best abilities. We want you to be happy here. We'd like you to gain skills and face challenges that will advance your career goals as well as provide you with appropriate compensation for your efforts. Now in order for me to do that, I need to know some things about you. For example, I need to know something about your previous job experience, maybe something about any self-development efforts in which you have been involved, maybe something about what you do in your spare time. Now, suppose you start by telling me about your previous job here with X and X Mills."

If in the first 10 minutes you do all the talking, you have taught the candidate that the way to do interviewing right, at least with you, is to listen while you talk. The most effective interviewing strategy is to have the candidate speak 80% of the time while the interviewer speaks only 20% of the time. Perhaps you are so delighted about what is happening in your own career that you want to share your excitement with the candidate. Untrained interviewers assume that it is important to tell the candidate all about the job at the very beginning of the interview.

From just 40 seconds of observation, without hearing the candidate say one word, a plethora of comments and evaluations were made regarding personality, mood, behaviour patterns, financial background, hobbies, political learning, age, state of health, birthplace, social status, educational attainment, motivation, eating habits, exercise preferences, ethnic, racial and religious background, leadership capabilities, integrity, honesty, sociability, loyality, dedication, detail orientation, open mindedness, obsessive compulsive behaviour, marital status, trustworthiness and ethics.

The purpose of the interview is to get relevant information about the candidate regarding a number of issues, like

- Competencies required for handling the work
- Interest in doing the job
- Ability to adjust to work environment
- Likelihood of being accepted by peers and superiors
- Probability of remaining with the organization
- Potential for growth and development
- Ability to articulate well

- Factors that might interfere with performance
- Level of maturity
- Clarity of judgement
- Sense of self-management and control

Any evaluation of what you hear must wait until the 20 minutes are complete. If you determine that the candidate is viable, then you continue the interview for an additional 20 minutes. An efficient and productive interview of suitable candidate therefore should take approximately 40 minutes.

Suppose you determine that a candidate does not have the skills needed for the job before the initial 20 minutes are over. Why should you prolong the discussion? There are two good reasons: The first has to do with public relations. An organization has a reputation to uphold in the community. It is important that potential candidates leave the interaction feeling that they are treated with respect and consideration. The second reason has to do with expanding the channels of recruitment. It may be true that this candidate does not have the skills and experience you require. People who work in the same type of occupation, however, know one another. If a candidate leaves the interview with a good feeling about you and your organization, it adds to your reputation. The idea is not to close off any potential avenues of good talent. In truth, good people are hard to find.

By dramatically altering your body language, you can end the interview gracefully. Here is how to do that. During the initial 20 minutes, make certain you give the candidate your complete attention with good, strong and direct eye contact. At the end of 20 minutes, lower your eyes to the candidate's paperwork, turning the pages over a few times while keeping your eyes on the papers. Then stand up (your eyes still on the paperwork of the candidate) and extend your right hand preparatory to a good-bye handshake while saying "Well, I guess I have all the information I need." Then raise your eyes to look at the candidate and say: "Thank you very much for coming in to see us. It was a pleasure to meet you. We have a number of other candidates to interview and should be ready to make a decision within the next few weeks. We will contact you at that time." With such body language and speech, there is no question in the candidate's mind that the interview has reached its conclusion.

Importance of the Candidate's Goals

The excellent time to cover the issue of goals is the first 20 minutes you are exploring all the details of the candidate's most recent job. If you decide this candidate is an excellent match for the vacancy, you want to be sure that the job offer you are going to make will be accepted. This is why it is essential that you discover something about the candidate's plans for the future and about the type of work environment in which the candidate feels fulfilled. The candidate has the answer to these issues; you don't. In this area, it is important not to make any assumptions.

When you ask about a candidate's goals, he/she will feel after the interview that you are sincerely interested in his or her plans for the future. That being the case, you immediately increase your chances 10 fold that any offer you make will be accepted. This is true even if the candidate has received an offer from another organization at a somewhat higher salary figure.

Here are some questions that will help you uncover the candidate's career goals:

- What do you expect to be doing in five years?
- In what way do you think this job will prepare you for that?
- What kind of experience or training are you looking for? Why?
- How will you know that we could provide you with that kind of experience?
- How would you know that this organization could make a real difference in your career by helping you reach your personal goals?

The following questions will assist you in discovering the kind of environment in which the candidate feels fulfilled:

- What are you looking for in a job?
- What would it look like if this organization could give you that kind of challenge?

- What kinds of efforts did you make to try to get those opportunities at prior jobs?
- What are the typical obstacles that have prevented other organizations from offering you those kinds of opportunities?
- If you could construct this job exactly the way you wanted it what would it look like?
- How would you determine if this was the right job for you?

Questions about the relevance of self development for the candidate:

- What criteria do you use to evaluate your effectiveness?
- When there are additional responsibilities available and you have to pitch in, how do you decide which extra assignment to adopt?
- Which job experience has added most to your development? How?
- In what areas would you like to become more effective?
- What are you doing to develop those skills?

In the last 5 minutes, you may want to ask about outside interests and hobbies. A candidate's response to such questions can sometimes lead into illegal areas, so this line of questioning can be risky. For example,

Manager: Do you hold membership in any professional or social groups or associations?

Candidate: I am the president of over fifty but we're nifty professional association, so a lot of my spare time is involved with those responsibilities.

In other words, a person who chooses to organize his/her spare time with solitary pursuits would probably prefer if allowed, to work alone rather than in a team?

Be aware however that whether a candidate is a loner or group-oriented is not always reflected in his/her spare time activities.

QUESTIONS AND SILENCE

Direct Questions

Direct questions require specific answers. They narrow the range of possible responses to a very few words — usually "yes or no". Examples are:

Manager: Did you like that job?
Candidate: Yes
Manager: How many people did you supervise?
Candidate: Eight

Direct questions do not give any idea at all of how the candidate thinks, makes decision, understands him/herself or perceives his/her environment.

The best strategy for you is to simply ask one question and leave it unrevised. Let the candidate struggle with it. Candidates are very capable of asking for clarification. Some will say, "What?" Others will ask, "Do you mean in terms of my work in general or with regard to this specific situation?" Still others will ask, "Could you repeat the question, please?"

Clarify the questions when you believe that what the candidate has just said is unclear or incomplete. There are two basic types of clarifying questions:

1. One asks for a definition.
2. The other asks for an illustration.

As an astute interviewer, you already know that the candidate does not use the words the same way you do. When you ask the candidate to clarify the meaning of what he/she has said, avoid making assumptions about what the candidate means. Delving into the candidate's superficial response with a few clarifying questions generally produces very worthwhile information.

Self-appraisal Questions

Ask candidates to analyze and evaluate themselves or their actions and skills. For example,

"What do you consider your greatest strengths to be?"

"What special skills and abilities would you bring to this job that other candidates would not have?"

Nevertheless, as an astute interviewer, you know that candidates come to the interviewer prepared with two lists: A list and B List.

The A list details all the relevant and favourable facts and attributes they want to tell you about the glorious reasons why you should ask them to become part of your staff.

But you may be more interested in the B list which contains negative issues that the candidate has sworn not to be dragged from his/her lips, even under severe stress.

Using Silence

It is nearly impossible in an interview situation for two people to sit there looking at one another in stone silence. According to a Harvard Business School study on communication, the maximum amount of time two people can sit in absolute silence is 21 sec. In the 22nd second, someone will speak. It should not be the interviewer.

There are two times in the interviewing process when it is vital to use silence. The first is after you ask the question. It is critical that you keep quiet and allow the candidate to construct his/her response. The worst thing you can do is trying to be helpful by either coaching the candidate, rephrasing your original question or providing a laundry list of response choices. When you do that, you have effectively derailed the candidate's train of thought. Self-appraisal questions especially cause candidates to become very busy mentally.

First, they have to figure out what the question meant: What is it that you are looking for and how does that relate to the job requirement?

Second, they have to put their responses together in words and phrases with proper syntax so that they sound convincing and competent.

The second time you want to use silence is after the candidate responds to your self-appraisal question. This time you will not have to wait for 21 seconds. All it takes is an extra 5 seconds of silence, and an additional flood of words will follow. After the initial 21 seconds of silence, you get the candidate's well-prepared, well-designated, well-worded and well-screened response containing items only from the A list. After the second silence of 5 seconds, you will hear items from the candidate's B list. So with just a little patience and silence you will see many candidates talk themselves right into or right out of the job.

There are three types of encouragements that you can use:

1. Oneword or two-word comments:
   Yes,

   Good,

   Hmmm,

   Uh-huh

   Interesting.
2. Direct requests to elaborate on what was already said:
   I'd like to hear more.
   Do go on.

   Please continue.
3. Use of body-language cues:
   Nod your head "yes" periodically .

   Make a small sweeping motion toward yourself with your hand.

A useful strategy to assist you with the spur-of-the moment question generation during the interview is called the hooking principle. This works by fashioning a question out of the last remark made by the candidate, using some of the candidate's words. Here are a few examples:

Candidate: Until that happened, I really hadn't given much thought to the importance of individual goal setting for my staff.

Manager: So why do you think that's important now?

The candidate's words may lie, but their body language always tells the truth. Immediately after the body-language reaction, the candidate's verbal response quickly follows. Two categories of bodylanguage cues are significant in the interview situation:

- The size of the physical distance between you and the candidate.
- The amount of continuous eye contact the candidate maintains with you.

Interviewer's Body Language

You want the candidate to understand that he or she is getting 100% of your attention during the interview. You also want to create a climate of positive acceptance —

that you will value whatever the candidate wishes to tell you and that you are not going to judge or criticize his/her life and career choices. All of those messages are conveyed through your body language .

Therefore,

- Give the candidate good, strong, direct eye contact,
- Do not sit back in your chair,
- In order to demonstrate that you are receptive to whatever the candidate chooses to tell you, keep your hands in full view, palms slightly open,
- A smile or a nod "yes" now and then doesn't hurt either.

Perter interviews the candidate at 9:00 a.m., Paul interviews the same candidate at 10:00 a.m. and Mary interviews the person at 11:00 a.m.

Unfortunately, because they have not adequately planned, all three will be asking the same questions. This is a big mistake. All three should have met at 8:30 a.m. to reassess the information needed according to the IIS. Then they should have decided who would ask what in order to avoid duplication of queries. At noon, all three get together to discuss the candidate. Peter thinks the candidate is not capable of handling the job. Paul believes that with a little coaching the candidate will be the best candidate. Mary has never seen such a talented candidate for this particular vacancy and wants an offer to go out immediately before some other firm grabs him.

A meaningful exchange will never happen unless you give up your mindset or mental context so that you can truly listen to the candidate and not the conversation going on in your own head. As a competent interviewer, first you need to recognize the candidate's context or mindset. Second, you must be able to communicate through the candidate's mindset and without the mindset of your own. This is quite difficult to do because every person is strongly affected by the presence of the other person with whom they are interacting at that time.

As interviewer you are now faced with three choices in terms of how to respond. You can parrot, letting the candidate know that you do not quite understand what he is telling you; you can paraphrase, putting what you have heard into your own words and asking for clarification; or you can interpret and feedback to him what you think you have picked up in his body language and tone of voice.

Research studies indicate that only 7% of the message is delivered through words while 93% is conveyed through body language and tone of voice. The share of the body language is 55% and that of the tone of voice 38%. If these statistics are true, they underline the importance of watching the candidate's body language throughout the interview.

Importance of Listening

Suppose you ask the candidate a perfectly clear and reasonable question, and the candidate's response is completely off the mark. You may attribute the mismatched response to the candidate's nerves or to your own laclk of verbal clarification. Correction is easy. You simply restate the question using different words. Now suppose this kind of misunderstanding happens a number of times during the interview. You would probably begin to wonder if there is something wrong with the candidate's communication skills.

Listening in the interview situation is an active rather than a passive activity. Because people speak at 150-175 words per mintue, and listen at 800 words per minute, there is a lot of time available for the listener's mind to wander. Good listening is a constant battle to stay alert and focused.

There should be no external distraction such as noise, telephones, interruptions, and so on. You must also ensure that there are no internal distractions either. Your mind should not be occupied with anything other than the candidate seated before you.

You can also use your own body language to help support the listening process and give the candidate your undivided attention. There is a formal listening position. Face the candidate straight so that you can establish and easily maintain eye contact. Sit slightly forward in the chair in an attitude of encouragement and interest with your hands on the desk in plain view. As the candidate talks, it is helpful to visualize the information in motion, as if you are watching a movie.

Listening through silence: Sometimes an interviewer will ask a question, anticipating that the candidate will answer immediately. Silence is not a negative attribute nor does it have to be filled with anything. You should simply let the silence happen, using the time to watch the candidate's body language, taking mental notes of the feelings and emotions that are being expressed physically. It is also good time to consider the direction the conversation is going to, and what information needs to be clarified.

Listening of learning channels: There are three channels on which people receive and process information—auditory, visual and kinesthetic. Although everyone has all three channels available to them, most people prefer one over the other two. According to various studies, 10-15% of the population prefer auditory channel, 30-35% kinesthetic channel and 50-55% visual channel.

A candidate who prefers the visual channel may make comments such as these:

"This looks like the right job for me."

"I can see what you're telling me."

"In view of the facts, it was not a clear situation."

"Can you give me a clearer picture of the responsibilities involved?"

A candidate who prefers the auditory channel may make comments like these:

"This sounds like the right job for me."

"Your description rings a bell; it sounds so familiar."

"She expressed her dissatisfaction loud and clear."

"Can you tell me again about the responsibilities involved?"

A candidate who prefers kinesthetic channel may comment such as these:

"This feels like the right job for me".

"I appreciate the fact that you laid all the cards on the table."

"I'm not following you. Would you please start again from scratch?"

"She could really get a person hot under the collar with her heavy handedness"

Listening visually increases the quantity of the information available for selection decisions by at least 100%.

As long as you are going to design your questions beforehand, it becomes fairly easy to rework a routine question into an exceptional one. There are four ways to accomplish this:

- Use numbers to make the question more quantitative.
- Ask the candidate to compare and contrast something.
- Request the candidate to analyze and evaluate different methods or strategies.
- Require the candidate to put him or herself in someone else's shoes.

Non-questions

To make the interview more conversational in order to create the feeling of a cordial conversation rather than an interrogation, try to alternate your questions with a more conversational, non-questioning approach. Here are several introductory phrases that you can put into the beginning of the questions that will present a query as a statement.

— *I'd be interested to learn.......*

— *Tell me about......*

— *I'd like to hear about.......*

— *Please compare the difference between......*

— *Describe for me......*

— *Please identify......*

— *Walk me through.....*

— *I'd appreciate if you could pinpoint when.......*

Just remember that when it is your turn to speak, say as little as possible that is enough to keep things going. That means that all you have to do is make an encouraging noise. There are several ways by which you can accomplish this.

- Encouraging comments: — *Yes*

  — *Good*

— *Uh-huh*
— *Hmmm*

- Words that convey intense interest: — *Oh no!*
  — *Unbelievable!*
  — *Good heavens!*
  — *Wow!*
- Starting sentences for the candidate to complete
  — *So what you realized was.......*
  — *And then you........*
  — *So the implication was.......*
  — *And in the end........*
- Divert requests for the candidate to elaborate on what he/she has just said
  — *I'd like to hear more about that.*
  — *Then what happened?*
  — *Please continue*
  — *Then what did you do?*
- Use of bodylanguage cues:
  — Nodding your head "yes" periodically.
  — Making a small "come on" sweeping motion with your hand.

Sometimes in the process of interviewing, you come across candidates who will attempt to creatively slide out of answering a question. Perhaps the question is difficult for them to answer. Maybe they fear their answer will open the door on some issue that would render them appropriate for the particular vacancy. Whatever the reason, your question goes unanswered. Instead, the candidate takes your words and fashions a different but related question out of them. Then he or she answers that manufactured question rather than the one you asked. If you are not listening attentively, you will miss the manoeuvre. If you grasp what is happening, simply repeat your question. Do not say, "You didn't answer the question". The candidate already knows that. It is not a revelation. Do not say, "Perhaps you didn't understand the question" and then restate it using different words. You already know the candidate understood your question very well. His or her body language tells you that; so the candidate is attempting to squirrel out of answering. Simply repeat the question over until you do get an answer.

Dumb Questions

These questions include those that have obvious correct answers as well as those whose only function is to take up space in the silence. There are four types of dumb questions.

- Questions that telegraph the desired response
- Questions for which the answer, although obvious, cannot be checked for truthfulness.
- Questions that offer a false choice of answers like the laundry list questions, except that there really is no same choice (if the candidate wants the job).
- Questions that serve no purpose except to give the interviewer a little mental time for question generation.

These dumb questions should never make it into your interviewing strategy. The problem is that such questions have a tendency to sneak in anyway. Should you find dumb questions creeping into your interview, the best thing to do is to stop for a moment and regroup your thoughts. Don't worry about the silence. Just take a few moments and consider what information you need to gather in order to make a decision.

Sometimes the signal for such free information is displayed through body language or verbal hesitancy. There may even be a change in the speed or and volume in which the candidate has been speaking. It is very easy to ignore the invitation to follow up. However, if you go after the additional information, you will gain some very valuable data. Here is a list of the invitations for free information to look and listen for:

- Unusually long pauses before answering
- Inappropriate use of humour
- Nervous giggle
- Overly complex answer to a very simple question

- Blushing for no apparent reason
- Abrupt loss of eye contact
- Immediate, heavy perspiring
- Quick and obvious changes in the candidate's body language
- Sudden change to more formal vocabulary
- Instant change in the tone quality of the candidate's voice (e.g. suddenly going lower)
- Body language that conflicts with the verbal messages.

KNOW THE CANDIDATE TYPE

The motivational need has the strongest influence over the candidate's behaviour and personality. During the interview, make shorthand notes on the candidate's motivational needs — with letter T denoting task; A affiliation and P power. Whenever the candidate says something that indicates a motivational bias toward task, affiliation or power, put an x in the appropriate column. At the end of the interview, you will have marks in all the three columns because people are driven by the combination of all three motivations but the majority of the marks will be in one column. Now you know which motivation is the primary driver of the candidate's behaviour. You also have a fairly accurate picture of the relative strength of the other two motivations.

Affiliation-oriented candidates will describe how they like people, that they have great human relations and get along well with everyone. Power people are certain to inform you about their leadership aspirations as well as their potential to move up in the organization. Whatever the message, the candidate will reiterate it in various ways throughout the interview.

Personality fit is not useful for determining professional qualifications, experience, probably longevity, skill set, learning ability or effective management potential.

Determining the personality fit needs of the vacancy.

(a) The manager's style of the boss (that's you)

(b) The nature of the work team already in place (your staff)

(c) The requirement of the job itself.

The personality fit "matrix" item should also indicate the combination of task, affiliation and power most likely to be successful in a particular position.

Task-oriented Candidates

They have a standard of excellence that far surpasses anything the organization will require of them. It is important for them to do everything right. To them, this means everything must be thorough. These people believe in leaving no stone unturned. They find a plethora of paperwork comforting. This is the candidate who will produce an eight-page resume with a sizable stack of reference letters at the interview. This is the only candidate who will ask to see the job description.

Task-oriented candidates tend to be perfectionists. The downside of this is that their perfectionism causes them to be intolerant of other's mistakes or lack of knowledge. In the interview, however, they will speak at length about the quality of their work, excellence in performance, and their personal high standards of honesty, dedication and ethical behaviour.

They prefer to work by themselves physically. They prefer an office with a door that locks from inside. No cubicles with a three quarter walls please. They have a low threshold for noise. They prefer to work in a situation in which the responsibility for results is attributable to their efforts alone.

They like to be involved in the genesis of anything — new procedures, creative ideas, innovative products, and unconventional ways of doing things.

Task-oriented people structure their non-work time around solitary or highly competitive activities such as tennis or bridge. For them, reading and surfing the Net are hobbies. Never will you hear about them being involved in a bowling league, alumni group, neighbourhood interest group or support group of some kind.

Affiliation-oriented Candidates

Affiliates are not motivated to work. They see the job as a social situation. In fact, they see everything as a social situation. This is the candidate who will enter your office with a big smile and immediately attempt to engage you in a personal "Let's make friends" conversation that has nothing to do with the interview.

You may ask yourself, "Is this candidate here for the interview or for my friendship?" The answer is: friendship first, interview second.

Affiliates will assure you that they understand the significance of going along in order to get along in the work situation. Affiliates may even bring a friend with them to the interview.

Affiliation-oriented candidates are not impedendent thinkers or doers. Affiliates gauge their behaviour by what others in the immediate area are doing. Affiliates' desire to be an integral part of their group is so strong that it seems as if they are unable to exist apart from that group. When asked what they liked most in their previous jobs, affiliates will speak about the people with whom they worked and of projects in which they were involved with others.

Affiliates find it difficult to adapt. They will make positive statements about everything you tell them, even when it is something negative.

Affiliates are so personable and friendly in the interview that they are a delight to interview. Speaking to them is like speaking to a close friend. You may not realize that your questions aren't really being answered. Their responses are shallow, and non-committal. If you ask whether they've had any problems on other jobs, the answer would be negative. In fact, they have never had a problem because mostly they get along well with others.

On the job, affiliates have a difficult time saying 'No'. Instead, they will agree to do what you ask and then conveniently forget about doing it.

Affiliation-oriented candidates will demonstrate relaxed and informal body language in the interview. These candidates like to touch. They will smile a good deal. It is typical for them to pull up the visitor's chair and reposition it so that the two of you are sitting at the corner from one another rather than opposite one another. These candidates have a preference for bright colours and patterns.

Power-oriented Candidates

A power-oriented candidate enjoys a leadership role and generally does very well with it. During the interview power-oriented candidates will express a preference for being in charge of things and/or people. These are the only candidates who want the organizational chart details so that they know who reports to whom.

These candidates enjoy working closely with those in authority, and if they have done so on previous jobs, they are certain to tell you about it in the interview.

These type of candidates describe their work history in such a way that it sounds as if they were the central — in everything with which they were involved, from project team efforts to establishing or changing company policies.

Power-oriented candidates firmly believe in the strength of their own abilities as a natural born leader. They are manipulative. You can never be quite sure whether they are sincerely interested in your job opportunity. Such a candidate may just be looking for an offer letter to use it to extort a sizable raise from his/her current employer.

These candidates have a sense of the image they wish to convey. If they know the company is looking for a business-savvy person, they will come to the interview with an expensive briefcase probably empty and a Wall Street journal folded so that the headline is prominently displayed.

Power-oriented candidates, like affiliation-oriented candidates, will demonstrate a relaxed and informal body language in the interview. A power-oriented candidate will never work up to his/her full potential. This is because he/she quickly learns exactly what he/she has to do to be considered good at the job, and that is all the effort you will ever get from him/her.

Whatever they do, power-oriented employees will make certain it is publicised and blown up out of proportion.

They may grab onto others' ideas and advertise them as their own.

You may see in them an overwhelming concern about status and reputation. They are generally looking for a job that will offer them more control over things and people.

KNOW THE LAWS

The term "protected classes" is used to identify those groups that are specifically protected by anti-discrimination legislation. Included are classes grouped by sex, race, national origin, religion, maternity, age (over 40 years old), handicap and military service.

Here are few examples of discrimination reflected job ads.

- *Wanted recent college graduate*
  Recent graduate means young, so this is age discrimination.
- *Wanted experienced, mature person for sales position.*
  Mature signifies an older person — age discrimination.
- *Wanted able-bodied person for construction work.*
  Able-bodied indicates that a handicapped person should not apply
- *Wanted native-born German for translation of manuscripts.*
  Stress on native-born German is discrimination by race and national origin.
- *Wanted drivers, must own car and have valid licence.*
  Owning car is discriminatory because it targets personal finances.
- *Wanted outgoing, congenial woman for restaurant hostess position.*

  Woman indicates sex discrimination.
- *Wanted male fitness trainer and instructor for city health club.*

Male indicates sex discrimination.

Here are a few good basic rules that promote sound and legal interviewing:

1. Treat all candidates equally.

2. If you would not ask a question to a male candidate, then you should not pose it to a female candidate.
3. Ask nothing about a candidate's personal life.
4. Focus on the candidate's skills and qualifications as they relate to the job.
5. Every question asked must have a direct and relevant relationship to the qualification required for the job.
6. Any measurement or parameter used to evaluate anyone for anything in employment is subject to equal employment opportunity (EEO) regulation.

EMPLOYMENT CONTRACT

Employment contract should cover

1. How work is to be done?
2. What results are to be accomplished?
3. The basis of the compensation offered.
4. The duration of the employment.
5. The territory allotted, for example, to a salesperson clearly delineated.
6. Description of the products to be sold. That leaves no room for disputes or claims.
7. A complete description of the duties of the salesperson:
   - Whether full time or part-time
   - Restriction on directly/indirectly accepting any other employment
   - Sales volume (quota) expected
   - Promotional activities
   - Customer-service activities
8. The compensation offered, including a clear statement of the salary, commission basis, and for drawing account, the time frame involved, and the payment of commissions after termination.
9. The paperwork to be done by the salesperson, such as the following:
   - Daily or weekly reports to be submitted by the salesperson.

- What those reports should cover?
- Identification of the point at which orders are considered accepted and commissionable.
- Details of how commissions are processed, when earned, and when paid.

10. The restrictions on the salesperson regarding price and quality concessions. A clear statement on whether the salesperson is to be bound by certain constraints regarding issues of price, delivery, quality or quantity.
11. The requirement of a fidelity bond, licence and so on.
12. The duration of the employment
    - If there is no stated term, the contract can be cancelled by either party anytime.
    - If the contract has a fixed duration, provide a specified time in which either party may cancel without cause and upon proper notice (30 days). This is known as escape clause.
    - Renewal clause
    - A statement that company retains the right to terminate for a cause (non-performance) or economic reasons (downsizing).
13. The collection of accounts — If the salesperson is to perform this function, a description of how it is to take place.
14. The restrictions after termination
    - Name of customers
    - Name of the competitor firm where the employee finds new employment.
    - Employment
    - Agreement period
15. How disputes are to be handled. This way it is quicker and cheaper.

OFFER OF EMPLOYMENT LETTER

The following elements should be included in an offer letter:

- The starting date of employment.

- The official job title that will be given to the employee.
- A statement that the company retains the right to terminate employment for any reason or no reason.
- A statement that this offer letter represents the complete understanding between the company and the candidate regarding the terms and conditions of employment.
- A statement that whatever is contained in this offer letter supersedes any oral statements that may have been made.
- A statement regarding the company's policy on discrimination and sexual harassment.
- A section concerning the terms of the probationary period, which also states that permanent employment is not necessarily guaranteed at the completion of that period.
- A list of the benefits that accrue with employment with references to appropriate manuals or documents that fully describe the extent and limits of those benefits.
- A place for you and the candidate to sign, signifying acceptance and agreement of the terms and conditions set forth in the letter.

The issues listed below should be discussed with the candidate prior to creating the offer letter. Although the following items can be included in the offer letter, it is not common practice to do so.

1. A list of the main tasks and responsibilities of the job.
2. The standards of performance for each task.
3. The conditions under which the tasks are to be performed.
4. Performance review periods.
5. Compensation adjustment periods.
6. Expectations regarding overtime and overtime compensation.
7. Policies regarding rest periods, lunch breaks, religious holidays, jury duty, national guard duty and family leave.

Section II

Dictionary of Organizational Behaviour and Human Resources

A

Absentee: One who is not present.

Absenteeism: Failure to report to work.

Absenteeism Policy: It is a policy that provides guidance within an organization as how to manage the state of chronic absence from work.

$$\textbf{Absenteeism Rate} = \frac{\text{No. of days absent}}{\text{Total no. of working days}}$$

(For job performance within the same level of job)

Absolute Measures: These refer to a method where performance ratings are based upon comparison of inputs of employees and fixed standard.

Abstract Intelligence: It is the ability of a person to understand and deal with verbal and mathematical symbols.

Acceptance Bonus: It is the bonus to be paid to the new employees when they join an organization.

Accident: A sudden, unexpected and untoward event which occurs in the workplace which may result in serious medical injuries to the staff or cause extensive property damage.

Accident-prone Worker: It refers to an employee who is more likely to have accidents than other employees.

Accident Report: It is a report of an accident which occurs at the place of work.

Accidental Sampling: It refers to the readily available cases that are taken by a researcher to conduct a study.

Accounts Payable: It is the money owed by a company to someone.

Accounts Receivable: It is the money owed by someone to a company.

Accrual Rate: It refers to the rate at which an employee's pension increases as every year of his/her service gets completed. It is the basis for calculating the employee's pension.

Achievement/Attainment Test: It is a test designed to measure the skills which someone is currently using. It is contrary to an aptitude test which measures the skills a person can use in future or at present.

Achievement Culture: *Trompenaars* defines the achievement culture as a performance evaluation system in which people are accorded status (job title or designation) based on how well they perform their functions.

Achievement Motivation: The degree or intensity of desire to perform as per the standard of excellence or to succeed in competitive situations.

Achievement-oriented Leadership: Setting of challenging goals by the leader for the subordinates with emphasis on high-level job performance.

Action Planning: The process by which employees plan to achieve their goals.

Action Research: The process of systematically collecting data on an organization, using it as feedback for planning future actions, then collecting more data to assess the results after planned actions have been taken.

Action Research Model: This model is based on the top-down approach. It lays emphasis on a rational, systematic analysis of the issue in question before taking action. To ensure the success of the action, the situation is analyzed correctly, all possible solutions are identified, and the one most appropriate to the situation at hand is applied.

Acute Stress: A short-term stress reaction to an immediate threat.

Adhocracy: It refers to the management which works by taking short-term decisions but fails to make long-term plans.

Adhoc Recruitment: The manner of recruiting employees without consciously following any one of the four recruitment approaches:

- Ethnocentric
- Polycentric
- Geocentric
- Regiocentric

Adjourning: It means dissolution of a group after achieving its goal. Many researchers call it the mourning stage. But this stage is never reached in permanent groups. These groups exist even after accomplishing their goals. Such groups follow the four-stage model of team development given by *Bruce Tuckman* in 1965. The four stages are:

- Forming
- Storming
- Norming
- Performing
- The Adjourning stage was later on added as the fifth stage.

Adjustment: It is the psychological process by which an individual manages to cope with various demands.

Admin: It refers to the administration staff or the administration department.

Administer: To organize, manage or direct the entire organization.

Administrative-level Need: It is the need of the organization to integrate its structural level with the technical system as well as with diverse work systems.

Administrator: A person who directs the work of other employees for any transaction.

Adventure Training/Adventure Learning: It is a type of training in which employees engage in group games and physically demanding outdoor activities away from their usual work environment.

Advisory Team: A team comprising individuals who get together to advice their organization on certain issues.

Affective Commitment (AC): An employee's emotional attachment or involvement with the organization.

Affective Culture: According to *Trompenaars*, in this culture emotions are openly and naturally expressed. In other words, in affective culture one needn't hide one's feelings as people do not object to display of emotions. Affective cultures may not give importance to the less explicit signals of a neutral culture.

Affinity Groups: These groups share common interests and can be good sources of feedback about the effectiveness of diversity initiatives. These groups can provide networking opportunities as well as career and emotional support to their members.

Affirmative Action: Also known as 'positive discrimination' or 'reverse discrimination', this action means consciously choosing those people for preferential treatment who have traditionally been discriminated against. This action aims at giving such people preferential access to education, employment, healthcare and other social welfare measures.

Affirmative Action Organization: An organization that is committed to remove some of the discriminatory practices which are inherent in the exclusionary and club organizations.

Age Norms: These norms relate the people's performance in a test to their age. These help in understanding many psychological characteristics which change over time, like vocabulary, mathematical aptitude, etc.

Agency Shop: It is an organization that requires employees to pay the equivalent of union dues even if they are not union members.

Aggression: It is the violent manifestation of anger expressed either verbally or through severe muscular movements. In the social psychological context, *Baron* and *Byrne* define aggression as a behaviour directed toward the goal of harming another living being.

Agile Organization: An agile organization is able to quickly adapt to changes. It can respond instantaneously to changing customer demands and pressures. The agile organization innovates rapidly, and immediately tailors products and services to customer needs.

Agreeableness: The extent to which an individual is easy-going and tolerant.

Alderfer's ERG Theory: According to this theory, the core needs of an individual or an organization are divided into three groups:

- Existence
- Relatedness
- Growth

Clayton Alderfer, who gave this theory in 1969, states that these needs are based on a hierarchy. He revised *Maslow's* theory of needs by reducing the number of gorups of core needs.

Alienation: Staff's negative involvement in their organization's work activities.

Alternate Form Method: This method relates to administering one form of a test (e.g. form A) to one group of individuals, and after some time administering an alternate form of the same test (e.g. form B) to another group of individuals.

Analytic Hierarchy Process (AHP): *Thomas Saaty* created the Analytic Hierarchy Process (AHP) in the

1970s. This system is useful because it combines two approaches: (a) The black and white of mathematics (b) The subjectivity and intuitiveness of psychology. Both these approaches are used to evaluate information and make decisions that are easy to defend.

Anchoring Bias: It refers to cognitive bias in which the first piece of information, encountered about a situation, is emphasized too much while taking a decision.

Annual Hours: Annual hours consist of variable hours worked each week and accumulated towards an annual total.

Annual Increments: These are effected in the basic salary and grade perquisites following annual review of an employee's performance.

Anxiety: *Freud* defines anxiety as an uneasy, fearful feeling, a specific unpleasant emotional state or condition of the human organism that includes experiential, physiological and behavioural components.

Application Blanks: These are heads like 'Name', 'Educational qualification', 'Experience' etc. in the application forms which are designed to gather such information about the job applicants that the personnel offices deem pertinent to the hiring process.

Apprentice Training: A formal apprenticeship to learn a craft.

Approach-Approach Conflict: This conflict occurs when an individual is motivated to approach two or more positive but mutually exclusive goals.

Approach-Avoidance Conflict: This conflict occurs when an individual is simultaneously motivated to approach a goal and de-motivated to avoid it. The goal contains both positive and negative characteristics for the individual.

Approval Motivation: It is the extent of an individual's concern about presenting himself or herself in a socially desirable way in evaluative situations.

Aptitude: *Freeman* considers aptitude as a combination of characteristics indicative of an individual's capacity to acquire (with training) some specific knowledge, skill or set of organized responses such as the ability to speak a language, to become a musician or to do a mechanical work.

Arbitration: It refers to the process under which a third party intervenes to resolve the dispute among the employees or between the management and the employees. It is similar to court proceedings and usually the last step in the grievance process.

Ascribed Status: It is the status and power assigned to an individual by cultural norms. It depends on the social position of the group to which the individual belongs.

Ascription Culture: According to *Trompenaars*, in ascription culture the status of a person is judged on the basis of who or what that person is.

Aspiration-Performance Discrepancies: These refer to the gaps between what an individual, unit or organization wants to achieve and what it is actually achieving.

Assessment Centre: It gives the candidates a better feel of an organization and its values so that they can decide on their own whether or not they are likely to fit in that organization.

Assessment Stress Interview: It is conducted to evaluate a candidate's ability to perform under a particular set of difficult circumstances.

Assessment Testing: It is the way of testing used to assist employers in pre-hire evaluations. These tests can be done via the Internet. They can provide employees with effective training, assist managers in becoming more effective and promote people into appropriate positions. They ensure that organizations place the right people into the right jobs.

Asset: It is anything of value that is owned by an organization or an individual. Cash, computer and investments are some examples of asset. An asset can be anything of value or real property or personal property that can be liquidated in order to pay the debts.

At-Risk Pay: It refers to the remuneration which varies across pay periods depending upon the level of performance.

Attendance Policy: The attendance policy of an organization contains guidelines for employee attendance at work. It is defined, written, disseminated, and implemented by the organization.

Attitude: An attitude is a hypothetical construct that represents an individual's like or dislike for an item. It often guides the person's behaviour. *G. W. Allport* defines attitude as a preparation or readiness to respond in a favourable or unfavourable way. Attitudes are positive, negative or neutral views of a person, behaviour or event. People can also be ambivalent towards a target, meaning that they simultaneously possess a positive and a negative bias towards the thing.

Attitude Interview: It is conducted to obtain information from the candidate about his/her attitude towards the job, company, etc.

Attitude Scales: These are psychological assessments applied to judge the extremity of people's attitudes.

Attribution: The way people explain the cause of others' or their own behaviour.

Attribution Theory: This theory is concerned mainly with the cognitive processes by which individuals interpret or attribute the behaviour of others or themselves. When they attribute their own behaviour, it is known as self-attribution. This theory explores how individuals attribute causes to events and how this cognitive perception affects their motivation. The Attribution Theory was developed by *Fritz Heider, Harold Kelley, Edward E. Jones* and *Lee Ross.*

Authoritarianism: It refers to the degree to which an individual believes in conventional values, obedience to authority and legitimacy of power differences in society.

Authority: It refers to the rights inherent in a managerial position to give orders and expect the orders to be obeyed.

Authorization Card Campaign: It refers to the situation where the employees or union members seek signatures from employees for union representation.

Autonomy: It means job independence. It explains how much freedom and control do employees have to schedule the work and make decisions.

Automobile Benefits: These are allowances given to the employees for the use of their own automobiles. These benefits may or may not be taxable.

Avoidance-Avoidance Conflict: It occurs when an individual is motivated to avoid two or more negative but mutually exclusive goals.

Avoidance Learning: It is the mental process by which an individual adopts a specific behaviour in order to avoid a stressful or unpleasant situation.

Awards: Awards, prizes and gifts are a traditional way of recognizing and rewarding the employees for their contributions by the employers. Such contributions may comprise long years of service, a cost-saving suggestion, a good safety record or outstanding performance.

B

Background Screening/Pre-employment Screening: This kind of screening ensures that the employers are hiring qualified and honest people. The screening involves criminal background checks as well as validating important information including PAN numbers, past addresses, age or year of birth, corporate affiliations, bankruptcies, and judgements.

Balance Sheet: It is the financial statement of a company or any other entity, showing what it owns (assets), what it owes (liabilities) and the owner's investment (share-holder equity) in the company at a particular time such as the end of the fiscal year.

Balance Theory of Group Formation: According to this theory, persons are attracted to one another on the basis of their similar attitudes toward commonly relevant objects and goals.

Banding Approach: It is the process of treating people as doing equally well when they have similar scores on a selection assessment.

Bargain Labour HR Strategy: It is a strategy that combines emphasis on temporary employees with a focus on reducing costs.

BARS (Behaviourally Anchored Rating Scale): It is a method of performance appraisal in which the employee's performance is evaluated against specific job-related behavioural dimensions of performance spread over a continuous range — from excellence to poor work.

Base Pay: Base pay is the salary fixed as per an employee's position in the organization and is paid for discharging responsibilities specific to his/her job. It is the remuneration which is consistent across time periods irrespective of one's performance.

BCG Matrix (The Boston Consulting Group): It was developed by *Bruce Henderson* of Boston Consulting Group in early 1970s, based on the product life cycle theory. It is also called BCG Model. Every organization should maintain a balanced portfolio of products, i.e. both high-growth products as well as low-growth products. Each product has a product life cycle and in each phase there is risk and gain. Four quadrants of the BCG Model show:

- *Stars* show that one should invest further. These ventures may incur high costs but at the same time, they also show promising gain.

- *Cash cows* show that one should keep the expenses (investments) low while keeping gains high.

BCG MODEL

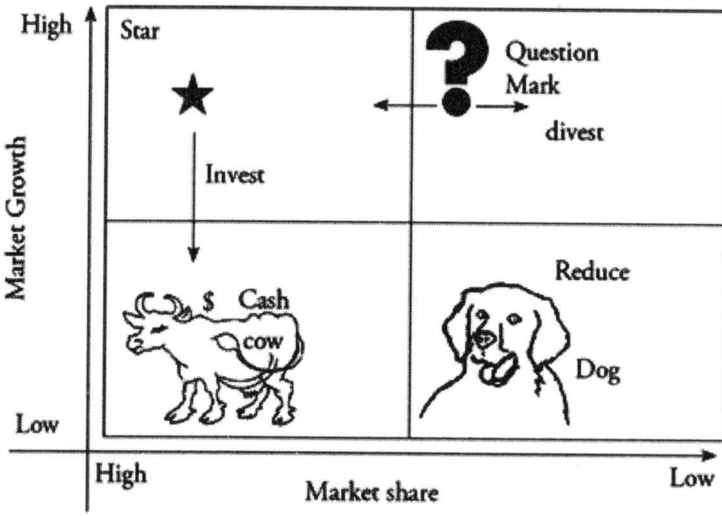

- *Dog* shows that if the investments are not delivering cash, one should reduce them.
- *Question Mark* shows that there is poor cash inflow; though there is high demand, return is low due to low market share.

Behaviour: It is the sum of responses, reactions made by an organism in any situation.

Behavioural Audit: In this audit, internal staff specialists and outside consultants would systematically analyze each job in question using job analysis techniques commonly employed in human resource management.

Behaviour Interview: In this interview, a candidate is asked to pinpoint specific instances of a particular behaviour occurred in the past.

Behaviour Modelling: It aims at improving interpersonal and communication skills through observational learning.

Behaviour Modification: This technique is used in clinical and educational fields to alter behaviour through both positive and negative reinforcements.

Bell-shaped Distribution: It is a normal distribution and also called the *Gaussian distribution*. It is denoted by a curve, called normal or asymptotic curve whose tail never touches the X-axis. Bell-shaped distribution represents an important family of continuous probability distributions, applicable in many fields. Each member of the family may be defined by two parameters, location and scale: the mean (average) and standard deviation (variability), respectively. It is often called the bell curve because the graph resembles a bell.

Benchmark Job: A standard job used as a base for making pay comparisons. It can be within the organization or in comparable jobs outside the organization. Employers can usually access various pay data through surveys.

Benchmarking: It is the process of comparing work and service methods against the best practices and outcomes to identify changes that, if effected, will result in higher quality output.

BEST (Building Effective Sales Technique): It is a short-term (generally five-day) corporate-driven training programme under which sales managers are trained in small groups. The aim of this programme is to impart practical selling skills to sales managers and teach them how to work as a team and build a network.

Big Five Personality Theory: According to *Goldberg* (1993), there are five dimensions on which an individual's personality is based. These are:

- *Extraversion* — It refers to a person who is sociable, talkative and assertive.
- *Agreeableness* — It refers to a person who is good natured, cooperative and trusting.
- *Conscientiousness* — It refers to a person who is responsible, dependable, persistent and achievement-oriented.

- *Emotional stability* — It refers to a person who is calm, enthusiastic, secure (positive) to tense, nervous, depressed and insecure (negative).
- *Openness to experience* — It refers to a person who is imaginative, sensitive and intellectual.

Biographical Data: This data, also known as bio-data, gives detailed personal information about a job aspirant, like age, sex, place of birth, place of residence, family background, number of brothers and sisters, education, work experience, physical characteristics such as height and weight, medical history, hobbies, pastime, and sometimes history of parents.

Blindspot Analysis: It refers to avoiding common fatal flaws in decision making. One way of doing this is to check your decision-making against a list of common blindspots. One such list was first drawn up by *Michael Porter* in his book "Competitive Strategy". The blind spots refer to obsolete thinking patterns (assumptions) which no longer hold true though they are still helpful in guiding any business strategy.

Body Language: It implies using one's body movements or gestures for communication in addition to or instead of verbal language. In body language, the facial expressions, gestures by hands, arms and legs, and postures are used.

Bonus: Bonus is a lumpsum award given to the employees based on the basis of the profits earned by the company. Bonus is usually paid on a periodic basis, i.e. quarterly, semi-annually or annually. Payment may be made in the form of cash or share or gifts.

BOS (Behaviour Observation Scale): This scale is used to assess the non-verbal behaviour. It is one of the appraisal methods which measures behaviour against levels of performance and also the frequency with which the behaviour occurs. It is used for evaluation in white collar jobs than blue collar jobs. It is often used to assess the behaviour of those suffering from autism.

Boulwarism: In negotiation, Boulwarism refers to an offer or counter-offer that is not meant to be negotiated. In simple terms, this is also called "take it or leave it" strategy. It is named after *Lemuel Boulware*, a former Vice President of General Electric Company, who would make only one offer in labour negotiations. Boulwarism is a highly aggressive strategy that may produce anger and frustration in the opponents.

Boundaryless Organization: This type of organization seeks to eliminate the chain of command, prefers to have limited spans of control and replaces departments with empowered teams.

Boundary Role: When an individual's performance depends upon others outside his/her immediate work unit, such a status may be thought of as a boundary status or role. The boundary role applies to the tasks that lie outside the domain of one's working area.

Boundary Spanners: According to *Daft* (1989), boundary spanning mainly concerns the exchange of information. *Daft* views boundary spanners as organizational members who link their organization with the external environment. Thus, a boundary spanner may be defined as a person who attempts to influence external environmental elements and processes. Individual decision-making processes influence the activities of boundary spanners.

Bounded Rationality: *Herbert Simon* has coined this term. He states, "Bounded rationality agents (employees or individuals in an organization) experience limits in formulating and solving complex problems and in processing (receiving, storing, retrieving, transmitting) information". Simon feels people are not rational – perhaps they are partly rational and partly irrational in their actions. *Daniel Kahneman* also proposes bounded rationality model against the rational models in economics where man is considered hyper-rational.

Brainstorming: It is a process in which a large number of ideas are generated in a meeting of those constituting a company's think-tank. However, the ideas are not evaluated for their effectiveness.

Broadbanding: It refers to broadening the pay grade thus reducing the possibility of overlap with other pay ranges.

Broad Skill Scope: It is a recruiting strategy that seeks to attract a large number of applicants.

Budget: An itemized plan of income and expenditure of an individual or company for a period in the near future.

Bureaucracy: Bureaucracy is characterized by highly routine operating tasks achieved through specialization, very formalized rules and regulations. In bureaucratic functioning, tasks are grouped into functional departments, centralized authority, narrow spans of control and decision making that follows a chain of command.

Bureau Pathology: Bureau pathology can be defined as the set of problems that arise from exaggerated bureaucratic controls. In other words, a bureaucratic structure can be said to suffer from bureau pathology when it is slow to change, strives to protect administrative roles, tends toward quantitative compliance and serves no role other than structural. Bureau pathology is justified by those who believe that the organizational procedure is an end in its own right, and not a means to an end.

Burnout: This term was coined by *Christina Maslach*. It refers to a state of complete mental, physical and emotional exhaustion. It can also be described as a syndrome of emotional exhaustion, depersonalization and reduced personal accomplishment.

Business Process Outsourcing (BPO): It involves giving the contract of the operations and responsibilities of a specific business function to a third-party service provider. BPO is often divided into two categories: (a) Front office outsourcing which includes customer-related services such as marketing or tech support. (b) Back office outsourcing which includes internal business functions such as billing or purchasing.

Business Strategy: It is a plan that a firm formulates and implements to succeed in competition with its rivals in a particular market that produce similar goods and services.

Buzz Marketing: It is a vital marketing technique that attempts to make each encounter with a prospective customer appear to be a personal, spontaneous interaction instead of an obvious marketing strategy.

C

CAI (Computer Assisted Instruction): It is an instructional method in which a computer is used to track an employee's or learner's performance and provide the presenter/trainer additional concepts to meet the learner's need in totality.

Cafeteria Plan: A plan in which an employer offers a variety of benefits to its employees. In this way, the employee is able to choose which benefits would fit his/her needs. The benefits offered may be group term life insurance, disability and accident insurance or reimbursement of healthcare expenses.

Career: It is a job or a series of jobs that one undertakes in one's working life for personal and occupational growth.

Career Development: It is an ongoing and formalized effort that focuses on developing enriched and more capable workers. It is not one-slot training program or a career planning workshop.

Career Pathing: It is a process where the employer and the employee identify job opportunities within the organization as per the employee's education, skills and experience.

Career Planning: It aims at developing and promoting high-potential employees in channels where their abilities will be used to the fullest.

Case Method: This method is used to teach students how to diagnose a problem and devise interventions. It is based on the tenet that management is a skill rather than a collection of techniques and conceptual knowledge.

Case Study: It is a written description of actual managerial problems, situations and events. It provides a simulation of various organizational problems facing managers on a daily basis. The origin of the case study method is attributed to the lawyers at Harvard.

Casual Wager: He/she is an individual whose employment is casual on hourly or daily rate basis.

Catharsis: It refers to venting of an emotion or 'getting it out of one's system'.

Centile Rank: It is the percentage of cases falling below a given point on the measurement scale. It can take values from 0 to 100.

Centralization: It refers to the degree to which decision making is concentrated at a single point in the organization.

Central Tendency Error: This error occurs when the employees in the middle range of performance are clustered in categories to avoid extremes. In other words, it is an error related to rating which places almost all employees in the middle of the distribution.

Chain of Command: It is an unbroken line of authority that extends from the top of the organization to the lowest echelon and clarifies who reports to whom.

Challenging Goals: They are better than relatively easy, mundane goals. However, these goals must not be so hard to attain, else their pursuit would be frustrating.

Change: It is a continuous, open-ended and unpredictable process of aligning and realigning an organization to its changing environment. It refers to the transition period between the two states.

Change Agent: One who indirectly or directly causes or speeds up change in social, cultural and behavioural spheres.

Change Management: It is the process of developing an effective strategy to engage change within an organization. Change management can be conducted continuously as a regular schedule or whenever deemed necessary on a program-by-program basis.

Channel: It refers to means by which a message travels from a source to a receiver.

Charisma: It refers to the leader's ability to inspire emotion and passion in the followers and to cause them to identify with the leader. It refers to an extremely charming trait marked by innate qualities of persuasiveness and communicability.

Chronic Stress: It is a long-term stress reaction resulting from ongoing situations.

Citizenship Performance: It refers to the employee's pro-social behaviour which creates a positive and conducive environment at work.

Classical Conditioning: It is defined as a process in which a formerly neutral stimulus, when paired with an unconditioned stimulus, becomes a conditioned stimulus that elicits a conditioned response. In other words, the stimulus-response connection is learned.

Classical Organizational Theory: It is characterized by an emphasis on structure, the framework that governs the interdependent parts of an organization.

Closed Shop: A closed shop is a business or industrial factory in which union membership is a precondition to employment. It is opposed to the open shop which does not consider union membership in hiring decisions and does not give union members preference in hiring.

Closed System: It is a system where innovative ideas for productivity and efficiency improvement are generated internally.

Club Organization: This type of organization is characterized by the maintenance of privileges by those who have traditionally held power. These organizations may technically get around the laws by hiring and promoting women and minorities. But they hire only those who are deemed to have the credentials and perspectives that appeal to the influential people in these organizations.

Coaching: It consists of ongoing, sometimes spontaneous, meetings between managers and their employees to discuss the employees' career goals and development in order to equip them with the tools, knowledge and opportunities they need to become move effective at work.

Coalition: It refers to a group situation wherein members act together to actively pursue common interests.

Coalition Tactics: It refers to seeking the aid of others to persuade to do something, or using the support of others as an argument to agree also.

Coding: It refers to classifying individual responses into categories. Responses obtained in a particular situation or context are classified into categories.

Coercive Power: This source of power depends on a person's ability to inflict punishment or aversive consequences on the other person, or at least to make threats that the other person believes will result in punishment or undesirable outcomes.

Cognitive Bias: These are the mental shortcuts involving simplified ways of thinking.

Cognitive Complexity: It refers to a person's use of and preference to elaborate intricate and complex stimuli and thinking patterns.

Cognitive Dissonance: It is a state of psychological tension aroused when a person simultaneously holds two ideas or thoughts—cognitions that contradict one another.

Cognitive Learning: It is based on the relationship between cognitive environmental clues and the expectations of a learner.

Cognitive Resource Theory: It was proposed by *Fiedler* and *Garcia* (1987). It focuses on leaders' cognitive resources i.e. their intelligence, technical competence and job related knowledge.

Cohesiveness: According to *Cartwright* and *Zander* (1960), it is the resultant of all the forces acting on all the members to remain in the group.

Collaboration: It refers to a group situation where a leader is not required and which is aimed at intellectual endeavour, innovation and creativity which happens through sharing of information and building consensus.

Collaborator: A person who is willing to work outside his/her defined role and share the glory with other team members. This person not only reminds other members of the vision, mission and goal of the team but is also quite flexible and open to new ideas.

Collateral Organization: It is an ODI (organization development intervention) designed to improve creative problem-solving by pulling a representative set of members out of the formal organization structure to engage in periodic small group problem-solving sessions.

Collective Bargaining: It refers to the agreements between employees and employers, which outline guidelines for acceptable work conditions including working hours, vacation, holidays and termination of service. These employees are typically part of a bargaining unit represented by a union.

Collective Efficacy: It refers to the capacity of the members of a group to share their performance objectives.

Collectivism: It implies an emphasis on the following:

a. The views, needs and goals of one or more in-groups rather than oneself.

b. Social norms and duties defined by in-groups rather than emphasis on behaviour that results in individual pleasure.

c. Beliefs and values shared with in-groups rather than beliefs and values that are idiosyncratic for particular individuals.

d. Readiness to cooperate with the in-group members.

Collectivistic Culture: Employees tend to show considerable commitment to their organization.

Commitment: It is positive involvement.

Committed Expert HR Strategy: It is a strategy that combines emphasis on permanent employees with a focus on producing innovative goods and services.

Common Information Bias: It refers to a bias in which group members overemphasize information held by a majority or the whole group while failing to be mindful of information held by one or few group members.

Communal Stage: An organization enters into communal stage after entrepreneurial stage that focuses upon expansion, creativity and cooperation.

Communication: It is process-driven. It refers to the exchange of information, thoughts and views between two or more people, according to *Shanon* and *Weaver* (1949). It is the transference of meaning and understanding of the meaning.

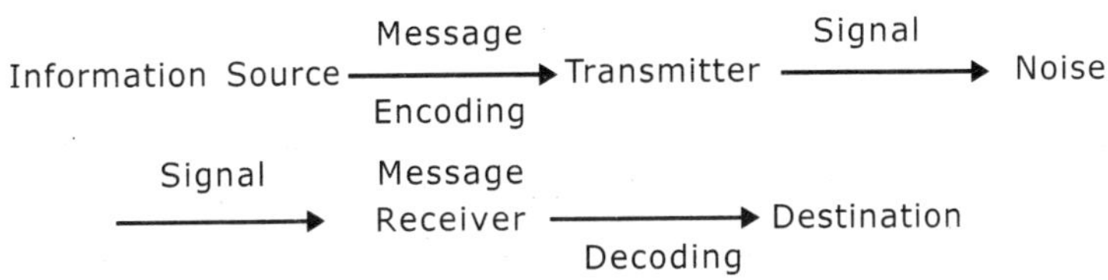

Communication Audit: It refers to an analysis of the organization's internal (supervisors and subordinates) and external (customers and vendors) communication to assess communication practices and capabilities and determine needs.

$$\textbf{Company Salary} = \frac{\text{Salary paid by the firm}}{\text{Average salary paid by competitors}}$$

Comparative Method of Performance Appraisal: This method requires the supervisors to compare the performance of the employees with their co-workers.

Compensation: It can be defined as an exchange between employees and organizations in which each is getting something in return for giving something. Compensation may also be defined as some form of payment for a service or product. It also refers to the sum of money given as remuneration, wage and salary, and the monetary help given at the time of work related injuries.

Compensation Management: It contributes to the overall success of the organization in several ways. To be effective, the managers must appreciate the value of competitive pay and their human resources, and have an investment view of the payroll costs.

Compensation Specialist/Remuneration Specialist: This specialist calculates employee compensation, maintains compensation database, develops job descriptions, benchmarks compensation externally and coordinates annual performance reviews. These specialists may also deal with employee benefits.

Competency: It is defined in terms of an underlying behaviour, skill or characteristic of an employee. It is a good indicator of success. It is a combination of knowledge, skill and behaviour required for performance on the job. Improvement in these will lead to improvement in performance.

Competency-based Approach: It is an HRM method that identifies skills and talents needed to perform a particular task to a certain standard. In the competency-based approach, a series of assessment tools are used to identify not only the technical skills of a candidate but also his behavioural competencies.

$$\begin{array}{c}\textbf{Competency Devlopment}\\ \textbf{Expense (CDE) per empolyee}\end{array} = \frac{\text{Total CDE}}{\text{Total number of full – time employees}}$$

Competitive Business Strategy: It is a strategy which focuses on different alternatives to provide goods and services that meet customer expectations and needs.

Competitive Goals: They are those goals toward which individuals aspire. Conflict management is very difficult when goals are perceived as competitive. Further, individuals seeking self-interest lead to mutual frustration.

Complete Finisher: A person who goes into every detail to tie up the loose ends.

Compliance: It refers both to a relation in which an employee behaves in accordance with a directive supported by another employee's power and to the orientation of the subordinated employee to the power applied.

Compliance Organization: An organization that is committed to removing some of the discriminatory practices which are inherent in the exclusionary and club organizations.

Compressed Week: It implies reduced number of working days but extended work hours in a week, that is, a work policy where the employee works for more than 8 hours in a shift or covers 40 hours of work which is usually covered during a five-day week.

Conceptual Skills: It refers to the mental ability to analyze and diagnose complex situations.

Concern for Production: It refers to one of the two dimensions of leadership behaviour of the managerial grid similar to the behavioural styles of initiating structure and job-centered leadership.

Concrete Intelligence: It is one's ability to understand and deal with things.

Concurrent Validity: It is practical because it is not necessary to select randomly or to allow a significant time-lag between testing and criterion measurement in order to obtain concurrent validity coefficient.

With concurrent validity, it is possible to obtain the test scores and criterion scores. Further, this is a parameter, used in sociology, psychology and other behavioural sciences.

Conflict: It refers to the process in which one party perceives that its interests are being opposed or negatively affected by another party. It arises when needs are opposed to each other.

Conflict Escalation: It refers to the process whereby a conflict grows increasingly worse over time.

Conflict Resolution: Conflict resolution refers to the resolution based on approval of either or both the parties. On the other hand, conflict management refers to the ongoing affair where the resolution perhaps does not take place.

Conformity: This term refers to the intentional change brought about by individuals in their beliefs or behaviour to identify themselves with a particular group.

Confrontation Meeting: It is an organization development intervention (ODI) designed to help determine how an organization may be improved and to start action towards such improvement. It was defined by *Richard Beckhard*.

Conscientiousness: It refers to the degree to which an individual focuses on goals and works towards them in a disciplined way.

Consideration-oriented Leadership: In the consideration-oriented leadership, the leader is supportive, friendly and gives importance to interpersonal relationships.

Constants: In a study, a particular characteristic cannot have more than one value. This single value makes the characteristic a constant, i.e. it can take only one value. Constants limit the applicability of the results of the study. They are such aspects of the experiment which are not under primary study but are inner environment and characteristics of the subject.

Construct Validity: It is the extent to which a psychological test may be said to measure a theoretical construct or trait. By construct we mean a hypothesis or an idea as defined and explained by the author or psychometrician. The examples of construct are: intelligence, anxiety, verbal fluency, neurotics, etc. These attributes are abstract properties of behaviour which cannot be defined in clear-cut physical terms.

Consultation Tactics: It refers to seeking your participation in making a decision or planning how to implement a proposed policy, strategy or change.

Content Validity: It involves systematic examination of the content of a psychological test to determine whether it covers a representative sample of the behaviour domain which is to be measured by the test.

Contingency Approach: It is a perspective that aligns different practices of managing people with different competitive strategies for producing goods and services.

Contingency Plan: It is a course of action to be followed if a preferred plan fails or an existing situation changes.

Contingency Recruiting: Contingency recruiters represent the outside organizations who do the frontline screening and searching for the talent. Contingency recruiting firms are not paid unless a candidate is successfully placed. They are unlike the contract recruiters who are paid for rendering services.

Continuance Commitment: It refers to an employee's commitment to continue with an organization due to his/her inability to bear the costs that he/she would have to incur on leaving the organization. It is also important because leaving the organization would cause the loss of his/her identity with the organization and sever friendly ties with co-workers.

Continuous Reinforcement: It is a reinforcement schedule in which a reward occurs after each instance of a behaviour or set of behaviours.

Contractual Employee: A contractual employee is one whose contract of employment is for a specific period and stands terminated automatically as per the terms of the contract.

Contrast: The contrast principle states that external stimuli that stand out against background or which are not what people are expecting will receive their attention.

Contrast Error: It refers to the error related to rating which unintentionally allows comparisons among employees to affect the ratings.

Contributor: It refers to a person who provides team with good technical information and data.

Control: In the field of research, the need for control is important in experiments. In an experiment, control is applied on those conditions which can give misleading results. Generally, factors other than independent variables are held constant. Without control, a researcher would have difficulty in determining the factors that brought about a change in the experiment.

Controlling: It refers to monitoring the activities to ensure that the activities are being accomplished as planned and to correct any significant deviations.

Convergent Thinking: In convergent thinking there is attempt to have different solutions that lead to the correct answer.

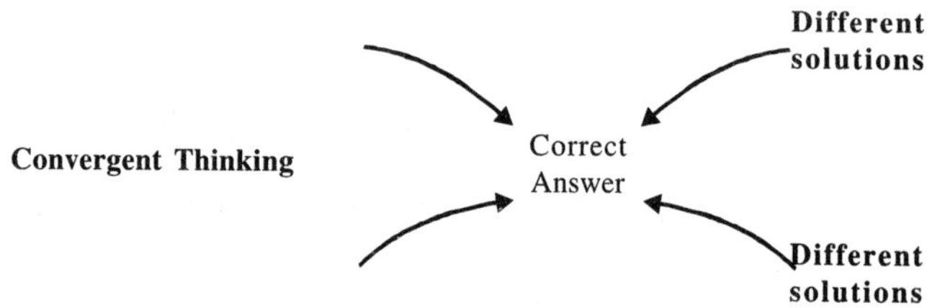

Cooperative Goals: Those goals which could be achieved only with the achievement of other members' goals. In other words, an individual can attain his goal only if other members of the group also attain their goal, as happens in a relay race.

Coordinator: He/she is a facilitator who organizes the efforts of others.

Corporate Culture: It refers to the custom of conducting business for that particular corporate house as to how people are expected to behave and the kinds of behaviour that get reward.

Corporate Strategy: It refers to the overall approach where an organization interacts with its environment and the emphasis it places on growth and diversification. Growth relates to increase in sales as well as associates and managers, while diversification relates to the number of different product lines or service areas in the organization.

Correlation: It refers to a connection between two or more things. Often in this connection one thing causes or influences the other.

Correlation Coefficient: It is a number that indicates how well the data points in a scatter diagram "bug" the straight line of best fit. In probability theory and statistics, the correlation coefficient indicates the strength and direction of a linear relationship between two random variables. In general statistical usage, correlation or co-relation refers to the departure of two variables from independence. In this broad sense, there are several coefficients, measuring the degree of correlation, adapted to the nature of data.

Cost Benefit Analysis: It is a relatively simple and widely used technique for deciding whether to make a change. It is often used in financial matters. Two things are taken into consideration: (a) Costs which are either one-off or may be ongoing. (b) Benefits which are most often received over time. By using both, a payback period is calculated.

Cost Leadership Strategy: It refers to the strategy that seeks to produce cheap goods or services.

Cost Minimization Strategy: This strategy emphasizes tight cost controls and avoidance of unnecessary innovation or marketing expenses to bring about price cutting for market competitiveness.

$$\textbf{Cost of Medical Allowance} = \frac{\text{Medical expenses on a particular disease or injury}}{\text{Total medical expenses}}$$

Cost per Applicant: It refers to the measure of recruiting effectiveness that assesses how much it costs to tempt each person to submit an application for employment.

Cost per Hire: It refers to the measure of recruiting effectiveness that determines the expense incurred to find each person who is eventually hired. These costs can include advertising agency fees, relocation costs and training costs.

$$\textbf{Cost per Trainee Hour} = \frac{\text{Total training cost}}{\text{Total training hours} \times \text{Total trainees}}$$

$$\textbf{Cost to Company Per Recruitment} = \frac{AC + CF + ER + TE + RL + RC + 10\%}{NR}$$

- AC: Advertising Costs
- CF: Consultant Fee
- ER: Employee Referral Costs
- TE: Travel Expenses
- RL: Relocation Costs
- RC: Recruiter's Time
- 10%: Administrative support which varies from company to company
- NR: Number of New Recruits.

Counselling: It is a form of communication between two individuals — the counsellor who is trained in counselling skills and techniques, and the employee who may require assistance in a particular area of concern.

Counselling Interviews: They help the employee with any particular personnel or job-related problem which might be harmful to his/her performance both on and off the job.

Counterparty Risk: It is the risk to which any party in a transaction is exposed to. It arises from the possibility that the counter party may default or fail to deliver its obligation.

Counterproductive Performance: It refers to the harmful behaviour of the employee towards the organization.

Country Risk: Risks that fall under this category are associated with lending or depositing funds or doing other financial transactions in a particular country. Among these risks are economic risk, political risk, currency blockage, expropriation and inadequate access to hard currencies. While assessing the country risk, factors like emerging market trends, location, history, current industrial base, unemployment and economic growth are taken into account.

Crafts Person: A person who holds traditional values, including a strong work ethic, respect for people, concern for quality and thrift.

Critical Incident Method: According to *Flanagan* (1954), this method involves the collection of a series of statements of job behaviour, based upon direct observations about good or poor job performance. Hundreds of thousands of incidents are collected from incumbents, fellow workers, former incumbents, supervisors and others. These incidents are then abstracted and classified into relevant categories. These categories give a composite picture of job characteristics.

Credit or Default Risk: This type of risk arises from the possibility that a debtor may not repay a loan (either the principal or interest or both).

Credentials: It refers to formal acknowledgement that a candidate has passed a particular examination (entrance tests + academic tests) or completed a specific field of study.

Criterion-related Validity: It is the validity of a decision that is determined by correlating the test scores and the measures of success or the outcomes of the decision. This correlation provides a quantitative estimate of the decision's validity.

Cross-functional team: It refers to a group of individuals from different functional areas (human resources department, finance, purchase and stores, marketing, etc.) and all levels of an organization and from outsiders (such as suppliers, customers, consultants and vendors in general) who work toward a common objective.

Crowd: It denotes a collection of persons who behave in a spontaneous and irrational manner.

Culture: It can be defined as the acquired knowledge that people use to interpret experience and generate social behaviour.

Culture Assimilator: It refers to a series of short episodes that describe inter-cultural interactions.

Culture Audit: It is a tool for assessing and understanding the culture of an organization. Culture audit examines the strengths and weaknesses of the existing culture in the organization with respect to its goals and objectives. It measures risk tolerance, creativity, beliefs and values, collaboration, extent of hierarchy and reward structure. It is a five-step process which uses interviews, observations, surveys, check lists and presentations to community stakeholders to evaluate the culture of an organization.

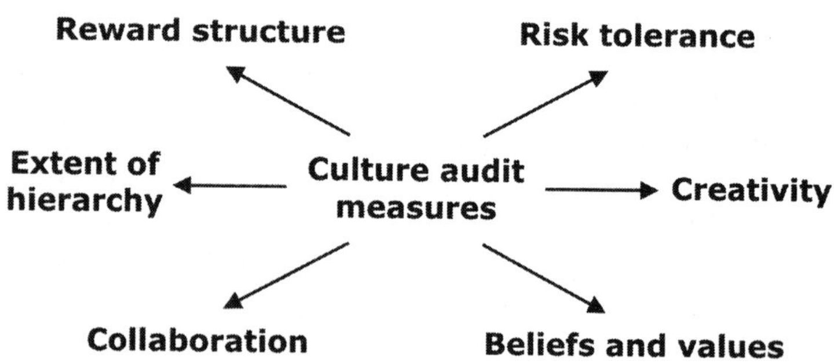

Culture Fluency: It is the ability to identify, understand and apply cultural differences that influence communication.

Culture Shock: This term was introduced by *Kalvero Oberg* in 1954. It describes anxiety experienced when an individual moves to a completely new social and cultural surrounding. It signifies a stress reaction produced by facing difficulties in coping with the demands and needs of life in a new country.

Currency Risk: It is a subset of market risk and is also called exchange rate risk. It is a form of risk which lies in change in the price of one currency against another. This risk usually affects the businesses, but it can also affect individual investors who make international investments.

Cybernetics: It is the scientific study of communication and control processes in biological, mechanical and electronic systems. Research in cybernetics often involves a comparison of these processes in biological and artificial systems.

D

DADA Syndrome: It is a sequence of four stages –

- Denial
- Anger
- Depression
- Acceptance

Through these stages an individual can move or he can become trapped when faced with unwanted change.

Death Claim: This is the process of obtaining a request for payment under the terms of a life insurance policy.

Decentralization: It refers to decision discretion which is pushed down to lower level employees. It relates to the removal of unnecessary levels, thus increasing the span of control, with more employees reporting to one manager. Line staff workers exercise authority, delegate more work and hold the employees more accountable.

Declarative Knowledge: It refers to factual information about a particular subject. An individual should have declarative knowledge before he/she can have procedural knowledge.

Decoding: It is the process by which the symbols are interpreted by the receiver.

Decision-making: It is an organizational process because it transcends the individual and has an effect on organizational goals.

Decision Trees: These are useful tools to choose between several courses of action. They provide a highly effective structure within which one can explore options and investigate the possible outcomes of choosing those options. They also help to form a balanced picture of the risks and rewards associated with each possible course of action.

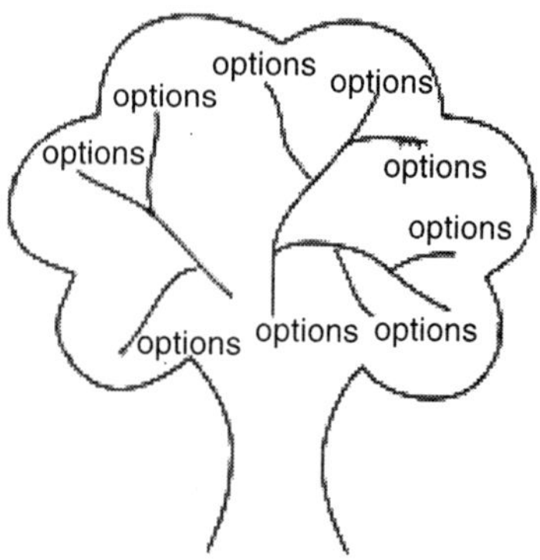

Decision Tree

Delegation: It refers to transferring formal authority from one level to the next level in an organization.

Delphi Technique: It was originally developed by Rand Corp. as a method of systematically gathering the judgements of experts for use in developing forecasts. It is designed for groups that do not meet face to face.

Delta State: It is the transition phase between where you are today — the current state, and where you will be tomorrow — the desired state. It is the space where change appears.

Deming Cycle: It is a planning model directed towards training and continuous improvements by integrating organizational learning into the planning process. It is a four-step (PDCA — Plan Do, Check and Act) problem-solving process used in quality control.

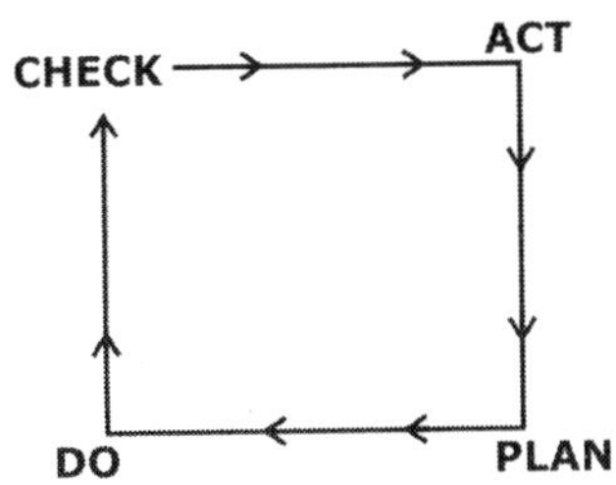

- Plan refers to stating the objectives in relation to specification.
- Do refers to implementing the objectives.
- Check means evaluating the processes and results against the objectives and specifications.
- Act means reviewing the entire process and modifying it before its next use.

Later Deming modified the PDCA to PDSA, which means Plan, Do, Study and Act.

The PDCA cycle was, in fact, originally developed in the late 1920s by *Walter A. Shewhart,* a Bell Laboratories scientist, who was Deming's friend and mentor and the developer of Statistical Process Control (SPC). So sometimes this is referred to as the 'Shewhart Cycle'. It is also referred to as 'Deming Cycle', 'Deming Wheel' or 'Plan-Do-Check-Act'.

Demand Control Model: It is a model stating that experienced stress is a function of both job demands and job control.

Demotion: When an employee is assigned to a position lower (in the company's hierarchy) than the employee's current position. This may be due to the result of poor performance, company re-organization or even at an employee's request.

Departments: These are the units in the organization which organize employees based on reporting relationships and code of conduct along with the kind of work associated with units.

Departmentalization: It refers to the basis on which the jobs are grouped together. In other words, organization is divided on the basis of departments such as sales and marketing, accounts, human resource, etc. Each unit performs a specialized job. It is closely related to the classical bureaucratic principle of specialization. On the basis of five dimensions, *Boone and Kurtz* (1993) have classified the departments in the following way:

- Process — Where departments are classified according to the steps performed in the production of an output.
- Product — Where departments are classified on the basis of the product being manufactured.
- Geographic — Where departments are classified on the basis of the location of the stores and branch offices.
- Customer — Where departments are classified on the basis of the type of interaction with different customers.
- Function — Where departments are classified on the basis of specialization in various areas.

Dependent Variables: They are the measures of the response of the organism. It is the outcome after independent variables have been systematically varied by the experimenter. A dependent variable is considered to be the main result of the experiment.

Depersonalization: It refers to negative cynical attitudes and feelings about one's client. It involves dehumanized perception of others which can lead staff members to view their clients as deserving of their troubles.

Descriptive Component of Female Stereotype: Females are considered to be emotional, weak, dependent, passive, non-competitive and low on confidence as stated by *Fiske, Bersoff, Deux and Heilman* (1991).

Descriptive Norms: These norms are indicative of what most people do in a given situation. It is different from injunctive norms.

Descriptive Statistics: It is concerned with the description of a group of individuals actually observed. The techniques of descriptive statistics are used to organize and summarize observations of a group of individuals actually observed.

Desired Organizational Culture: It is rooted in the shared expectations of the organizational members about values and behavioural standards in an organizational context. It is related to 'what should be'.

Deviation Score: It expresses the location of a score by indicating how many score points it lies above or below the mean of the distribution.

Deviation score can be defined as:

x = (X-X^)

Devil's Advocacy: It is a group decision-making technique that relies on critiques of single sets of recommendations and assumptions to encourage full discussion. If compared with consensus, it is seen as a high conflict decision-making process. Devil's advocacy enhances decision making in disjunctive tasks and retards decision making in additive tasks, and has no effect on conjunctive tasks. A group's atmosphere is more positive in consensus groups.

Dialectical Inquiry: It is a group decision-making technique that uses debate between highly different sets of recommendations and assumptions to encourage full decision. It is a method resembling devil's advocacy approach. It is a more balanced and conducive approach. *Aristotle* states that dialectics deal with an upright looking for truth.

De Wit and *Meyer* emphasize dialectical inquiry over strategic paradoxes. They say that critical ideas can be discussed, exploiting a range of ideas, providing a stimulus that bridges the irreconcilables.

Dictionary of Occupational Title (DOT): It is one in which 75,000 jobs were studied and came with 20,000 jobs prepared by the Bajaj Institute of Management. This DOT is a nine-digit code. The first three digits describe the occupational category. The next three digits relate to the functions to be performed and the last three digits represent titles or positions.

Differentiation Strategy: It refers to the strategy that seeks to produce superior quality of goods or services in comparison to what is produced by competitors, and customers are willing to pay a higher price for them.

Difficult, Challenging Goals: They are better than relatively easy, mundane goals. However, these goals must be reachable even though their pursuit could be frustrating.

Diffuse Culture: It is one in which both public and private space are similar in size, and individuals guard their public space carefully because entry into public space affords entry into private space as well.

Directive Leadership: It is one in which the leader should tell the subordinates what they should do and how they should do it.

Disability Insurance: It is a form of compensation made to the individual who develops some psychological or physical disability which debars the individual from normal functioning.

Discrimination: Disparate or unequal treatment of employees unrelated to qualification, skills or performance on the basis of race, religion, gender, etc.

Disengagement: It is the fourth and final career stage in which the individual gradually begins to pull away from work in the organization, priorities change and work may become less important.

Disparate Treatment: It refers to differential treatment to employees based on race, sex, religion, etc.

Displacement: In displacement, the motive remains unaltered but the person substitutes a different goal object for the original one.

Distance Learning: It is an upcoming field of education which is based on pedagogy type of technology that is suitable in delivering education to learners who are not present on the site of teaching physically.

Distress: It is a negative stress and is referred to simply as stress.

Distributive Bargaining: It assumes a 'fixed pie' and focuses on how to get the biggest share or 'slice of the pie'. It refers to the process which is used in negotiation where there is something to divide.

Distributive Justice: It is perceived fairness of the amount and allocation of rewards among individuals.

Divergent Thinking: It refers to a person's ability to generate novel, yet appropriate responses to questions and problems. In divergent thinking people throw ideas in a random manner in order to have as many ideas in a short period of time and to gain insight about different aspects of the problem.

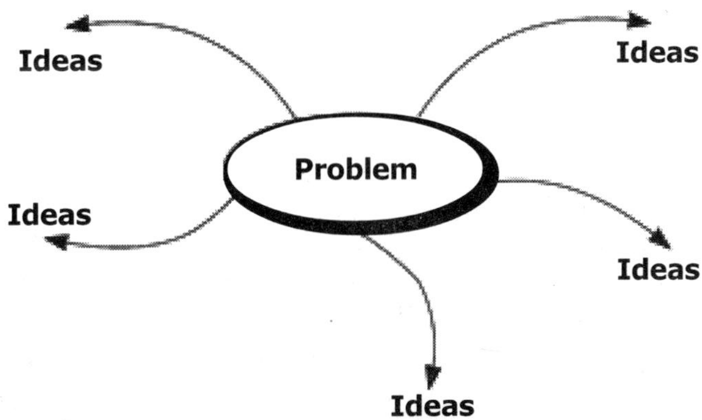

Divergent Thinking

Diversification: It relates to the number of different product lines or service areas in the organization.

Diversity: *R. Roosevelt Thomas* has conceptualized the meaning of diversity on micro and macro continuum.

- A micro perspective looks at the individual component.
- A macro perspective looks at the mixture.

To get to the true nature of diversity (comprising differences and similarities), an ability to assume both perspectives simultaneously is required; the micro facilitates the identification of differences and the macro enhances the ability to see similarities.

Diversity Management: It is not simply a mutual adaptation but is the process of responding appropriately to diversity mixtures. These diversity mixtures are of people discriminated on the basis of race, religion, region and sex.

Divisible Tasks: These are the tasks that can be separated into subcomponents.

Documental Analysis: It refers to the review of records from Training and HR and HR manual.

Domain Planning: It is the development of the course of action that moves the organization towards one area of planning or away from other areas of planning.

Dominant Values: These are major values that the organization advocates and expects the employees to share.

Downsizing: It refers to the reduction of the number of employees in the workforce. This is usually an effort made by the company to reduce or eliminate inefficiencies or duplication of efforts.

Downtown Hotel: It may be situated in the centre of the city, along with shopping areas, theatres and public buildings.

Downward Communication: It is a process where the flow is from the top management to the worker level. It is the communication that flows from top to bottom.

Drive: It is a tendency to behave in a manner that corrects an organic need.

Drug Testing: Testing of usually a urine sample for substance abuse.

Dual-Career Couple: A situation for a couple where both the members have occupational responsibilities and career issues at stake.

Duty: It is a general term that is sometimes used loosely to cover a broad group of related tasks. It is a result of one's moral expectations and one's personality. It is a result of being human.

Dysfunctional Conflict: It is the conflict that is detrimental to organizational goals and objectives.

Dysfunctional Turnover: It is a situation where good employees choose to leave the organization.

E

EAP (Employee Assistance Program): It is a counselling program for employees which enables them to deal with personal or work-related problems.

Earnings: These are the total wages or the cash earned within a specific period of time. These include base pay, premium, overtime and bonuses.

Ease of Recall Bias: It is a cognitive bias in which information that is easy to recall from memory is relied on too much in making a decision.

E-commerce: It focuses on distributing, meeting demands, marketing and servicing of both products or services over the Internet and other computer systems.

Economic Man Theory: The economic man was used by *John Stuart Mill* while working on political economy. In some economic theories, it is the concept of man as a rational and proactive individual who works towards attaining wealth and avoids unnecessary labour.

Education: It refers to formal education received from a school, college or university.

Education and Training Trends: These trends concern the knowledge and skills that employees will require in the future.

EEO (Equal Employment Opportunities): These are provided to ensure that the employees are protected from any unlawful discrimination and to overcome any past or present disadvantage.

Effectance Motivation: It is a motive to act competently and effectively when interacting with the environment.

Effectiveness: It refers to the achievement of goals.

Efficiency: Efficiency is the ratio of the effective output to the input required to achieve it.

EI (Emotional Intelligence): It describes an ability, capacity or skill to perceive, assess and manage the emotions of one's self, of others and of groups. According to *Steven:*"EI refers to an innate ability which gives us our emotional sensitivity and our potential for learning healthy emotional management skills."

EIS (Executive Information System): It facilitates decision making by providing information which is important for meeting strategic goals of the organization.

Elaboration Stage: It is the last and final stage in the organization life cycle. It focuses on renewal and adaptation which is similar to the middle age of human beings.

E-learning: It refers to training delivered through computers via the Internet.

Electronic Advertising: It refers to the use of electronic ways of communication such as the Internet and cell phones.

E-mail Technique: It can be used only on a selected sample. It doesn't reflect the opinion of a representative population. It is a quick way of getting responses.

Emergent Leader: An individual who becomes a leader by virtue of internal processes and dynamics of the group. Emergent leaders are becoming popular because of flattening of the organizational structure and increase in the number of virtual teams. Emergent leaders are also defined as group members who exert significant influence over other members of the group. However, no formal authority is vested in an emerging leader (*Schneider and Goktepe, 1983*).

Emergent Leadership: It has been defined as a dynamic social process during which a specific individual adopts the role of leader (*Moss and Kent,* 1996). Emergent leadership has been considered to be a leadership substitute, which occurs in situations where a formal leader is absent, yet where a leadership role must be fulfilled to accomplish performance requirements (*Lawler,* 1988). Although the definitions of emergent leadership vary, they do share the common theme that emergent leadership is a social process, whereby its occurrence is dependent upon the individual, the followers, the situation, or an interaction among these components.

Emotion: According to *Klienginna and Kleinginna*, (1981) emotion is a term that refers to the following:

- Should say something about the way we feel when we are emotional.
- Mention the physiological basis of emotion.
- Include the effects of emotion on perception, thinking and behaviour.
- Point out the motivational properties of certain emotions such as fear and anger.
- The ways in which emotions are expressed in language, facial expressions and gestures.

Emotional Exhaustion: It refers to a situation where emotional resources are depleted and workers feel that they are no longer able to give themselves at a psychological level.

Emotional Stability: The emotional stability of an individual is the degree to which the individual is able to handle stressful situations and heavy demands easily.

Emotional Stress: It is the stress that results when people consider situations difficult or impossible to deal with.

Employee Advocate Role: This role is about maintaining the interests of employees and ensuring that they are fairly treated.

Employee and Labour Relations: These focus on building a congenial relationships between employers and employees.

Employee Benefits: These are the forms of compensation (excluding cash) available to the employees. Benefits include health coverage, vacation, income protection, retirement savings, etc. Number and types of benefits vary for each organization.

Employee-centred Leadership Style: This is a leadership behavioural style that emphasizes employee's personal needs and the development of interpersonal relationships.

$$\textbf{Employee Involvement Index (EII)} = \frac{\text{Number of satisfied}}{\text{Number of employees participated in survey}} \times 100\%$$

Employee Retention: It focuses on retaining employees from leaving the organization.

Employee Self-service: It is a programme that allows employees to handle many job-related tasks normally conducted by HR departments including benefits, enrollment as well as updating personal information. Employees can access the information through the company's intranet, cyber cafes, or other web-based applications.

Employee Separation: It focuses on terminating the services of an employee.

Employee Turnover: It corresponds to the situation where the employees leave the organization and new employees take over the positions left by the leaving employees.

Employment Agency: It is a firm that provides a platform for employment to match an individual's job needs. The first employment agency was opened by *Fred Winslow* in the USA in 1893. It was an engineering agency.

Employment Branding: It is a strategy which makes an organization appealing to its employees as a good place to work.

Employment Opportunity Trends: It refers to the trends concerning the new types of jobs that will occupy the employment market in future.

Empowered Team: It is a team characterized by collective efficacy, meaningfulness, independence and ability to influence.

Empowerment: Empowerment is the result of a process that enhances feelings of self efficacy among organizational members, enabling them to feel as though they can perform their work effectively and that they are responsible for doing so. Critics regard empowerment in the work place as "pseudo empowerment". The idea is to change the perception in employees so that they work harder without giving them the actual power. *Wilkinson* (1998) calls it Attitudinal Shaping.

Encoding: It is the process of transforming the intended message into symbols used to transmit.

Entrepreneurial Stage: It corresponds to that stage where the organization is formed and focuses on survival and growth.

Environmental Frustration: The obstacles from the environment can thwart the individual from attaining his/her goals.

Environment: It refers to those institutions or forces outside the organization that potentially affect the organization's performance.

EPPA (Employee Polygraph Protection Act): This act protects the employees from undertaking a lie detector test, arranged by the employer, either for pre-employment screening or during the course of employment.

Episteme: It is the universal knowledge which we share and circulate and which we teach and preserve and what is commonly understood by the firms as their heritage.

Equity Theory: Social psychologist *J. Stacy Adams* argues that a major input into job performance and satisfaction is the degree of equity or inequity that people perceive in their work situation.

$$\text{Degree of Equity: } \frac{\text{Person's outcomes}}{\text{Person's inputs}} = \frac{\text{Others' outcomes}}{\text{Others' inputs}}$$

E-recruitment: The recruitment services provided over the Internet are called e-recruitment. They offer the opportunity for the job-seekers to log in and post their resumes. Similarly, different organizations post their job-openings with these online services, using e-mail and chart-boards for further communication. Typically, the Internet Service Provider charges the organization a fee for posting the open position information.

Ergonomics: It refers to a methodical application of known information about every aspect (physical, psychological and social attributes) of human beings to the establishment and use of everything that may affect a person's working condition. This includes working environment, layout, training, organization of the workload and the job itself.

ESOP (Employee Stock Ownership Plan): It is an arrangement whereby employees may or may not be the exclusive owners of the organization. Ownership is frequently the result of an employee-ownership having been established by the company on the employee's behalf. It is a corporate finance plan which aims to align the company's employees with the company's shareholders. Here the participants themselves are shareholders, therefore they can watch down on what is best for shareholders and how the company's stock performs well.

Essay Method: This is a method of Performance Appraisal. It requires the rater to write a paragraph about the employee's performance, training received and required, strengths, and areas that require improvement.

Establishment: It is the second career stage which involves creating a meaningful and relevant role in the organization.

Esteem for the Least Preferred Co-worker (LPC) Questionnaire: It is a questionnaire used with Fiedler's Contingency Model of Leadership Effectiveness to assess the leadership style in terms of how task-oriented or relationship-oriented a leader is.

Ethics: Ethics are a set of standards that mark what is right and wrong, and promote parity in human actions.

Ethnocentrism: It refers to the belief that one's culture is better than others. It is the sense of superiority that members of a particular culture have.

Ethnocentric Approach: It refers to the key positions in a multicultural firm being filled by the parent country nationals.

Ethnographic Interviewing: It allows the researcher to hear directly from employees about how they interpret their experiences in the organization, their interpersonal dynamics with superior colleagues and peers along with interpretations of the efficiency and inefficiency of the processes operating within the organization. It is conducted in order to study how every employee's experience is located in a context, in terms of policies of the organization.

Eustress: It is the positive stress that results from meeting challenges and difficulties with the expectation of achievement.

Evolutionary Strategic Approach: It refers to the situation where the strategies of an organization unfold over a period of time in response to day-to-day issues. This is not always planned.

Exchange Tactics: These refer to making explicit or implicit promises that a person will receive rewards or tangible benefits if he/she complies with a request or support a proposal. It also includes reminding of a prior favour to be reciprocated.

Exclusionary Organization: This type of organization is the furthest from a multicultural organization. It is devoted to maintaining the dominance of one group over all others on factors such as age, education, gender or race.

Exclusive Groups: These are the groups that limit their membership to certain classes of individuals.

Executive Delay: It means that the executive has correctly guessed the future state of affairs but he decides not to take actions.

Executive Delight: It means that the executive has correctly guessed the future state of things and has decided to act.

Executive Fright: The executive incorrectly guessed the future state of things and has decided to act according to his incorrect predictions. Since his action will thus turn out to be inappropriate as he has guessed wrong, this is termed as the executive fright.

Executive Stays: The executive has not only incorrectly guessed the future state of events but also failed to act on his prediction and has simply stayed in his present situation.

	Executive takes no action	Executive takes action
Executive Hypothesis is correct	Executive Delays	Executive Delight
Executive Hypothesis is false	Executive Stays	Executive Fright

Exit/Separation Interview: It refers to one-to-one discussion between the management and the employee to know why an employee wants to quit the organization.

Expatriate: It refers to an individual who leaves his/her home country to live and work in a foreign land for a definite period of time.

Expectancy: It refers to the subjective probability of that effort which will lead to performance.

Expectancy Effect: It occurs when people perceive stimuli in ways that will conform to their expectations.

Expectancy Theory: It is a theory of motivation suggesting that individuals get motivated by an interplay of valence, instrumentality and expectancy. Instrumentality refers to the belief that the reward/incentive is contingent on good performance. Expectancy refers to the belief that the necessary action is needed to perform well.

Expected Norms: These are the traditional norms which are expected within the group.

Experiential Groups: These are the groups where individuals seek to improve their own skill or lifestyles through participation in the group, according to *Shaw* (1981).

Expert Power: This power was identified by *French* and *Raven*. It is based upon the extent to which other people attribute knowledge and expertise to the power seekers.

Explicit/formal: These are precisely stated and enforced rules, as in case of a written constitution, by law or recorded laws governing conduct.

Explicitness: It is the quality of clarity and lucidity.

Exploration: It is the first traditional career stage and involves identifying interests and opportunities.

External Equity: It is the perception of an employee about fairness based on how much he is paid relative to people working in other organizations.

External Labour Orientation: It is a perspective that focuses upon hiring workers who possess skills that are needed to do specific tasks.

External Locus of Control: It refers to the individuals who believe that things such as fortune, events, people and organization in which they work are the primary determinant of their behaviour.

External Priming: It refers to the receiving of cues from others.

External Sourcing: It is a recruiting strategy that recruits people from outside the organization where the job vacancy exists.

Extinction: It is a reinforcement contingency in which a behaviour is followed by the absence of a previously encountered positive consequence, thereby reducing the likelihood that the behaviour will be repeated in the same or similar situations.

Extraneous Variables: Extraneous variables are variables other than the independent variables that may bear any effect on the behaviour of the person being studied. These are of three types:

- Subject variables are the characteristics of the individuals being studied that might affect their actions. These variables include age, gender, health status, mood, background, etc.
- Experimental variables are the characteristics of the persons conducting the experiment which might influence how a person behaves. Gender, presence of racial discrimination, language, or other factors may qualify as such variables.
- Situational variables are features of the environment in which the study or research was conducted, and these have a bearing on the outcome of the experiment. These variables include air temperature, level of activity, lighting, and the time of day.

Extraversion: It refers to the degree to which an individual is outgoing and derives energy from being around other people.

Extrinsic Motivation: It occurs when a person performs a given behaviour to acquire something that will satisfy a lower order need. Extrinsic motivation focuses people's efforts on rewards than on action.

Extrinsic Rewards: These rewards are related to work and they are received for the performance that can be measured in monetary terms.

F

Face Validity: It refers not to what the test actually measures but to what it superficially appears to measure. It pertains to whether the test looks valid to the subjects who take it, the administrative personnel who decide on its use and other technically untrained observers.

Factor Analysis: It is a statistical technique that helps to identify combinations of job variables that tend to go together. The combinations of such inter-related variables are called factors or job dimensions in the field of job analysis.

Family-to-work Conflict: Meeting family obligations causes some problems to arise which negatively influence work and performance.

Feedback: It refers to the objective information about progress and performance. It can come from the job itself or from supervisors or through an information system. Feedback tells us whether or not the message had the intended impact on the audience.

Feedback Specificity: It refers to the extent of details in the feedback information — from information about the overall performance of the employee to specific information about the employee's behaviour.

Femininity: It refers to the characteristics and behaviours that are appropriately related to the feminine gender.

Field Experiment: It was given by *Kerlinger*. It is a study done in natural setting in which one or more independent variables are manipulated by the experimenter under as carefully observed conditions as the situation permits. For example, office, playground or working situation.

Field Notes: These notes refer to a form of representation, i.e. a way of turning the just-observed events, persons and places to the written accounts.

Filtering: It refers to a sender who manipulates the information so that the information may be seen more favourably by the receiver.

$$\textbf{Financial Staff over Total Staff} = \frac{\text{Total number of employees in the finance department}}{\text{Total number of employees}} \times 100\%$$

First Shift Rule: In this scheme, the group tends to adopt a decision that reflects the first shift in opinion expressed by any group member.

Fish Bowl Exercise: It is a method which involves participants to observe others and provide objective feedback and also learn about themselves as seen through the eyes of others, enabling them to improve their strengths and overcome weaknesses.

It is one of the off-job techniques. It is conducted for the following purposes:

- To understand human behaviour.
- To inculcate the discipline of observing others in the participants, and on the basis of this learning provide an objective and constructive feedback.
- To study the content of communication.
- To understand the dynamics of group problem-solving and decision-making and interpersonal relations.

Fixed Alternative Method: In this method, the options in which the respondent has to answer, are fixed.

Fixed Pay: Fixed pay is the remuneration which is not based upon performance. It is a non-discretionary compensation which does not vary due to performance. In other words, it is a salary which is paid after a month from the employer to the employee.

FJA (Functional Job Analysis): It is a task-related job analysis. It is done in terms of worker's functions. It was developed by *Sidney Fine et al* (1944). Worker functions are activities that identify the worker relationships with data, people and things. Work elements are scored in terms of 0-6 in data, 0-8 in people and 0-6 in things.

The most recent version of FJA uses seven scales to describe what workers do in jobs –

1. Things
2. Data
3. People
4. Worker Instructions
5. Reasoning
6. Maths
7. Language

Flat Organization: An organization that incorporates wide spans of control.

Flexi-time: It includes concepts like annual hours, compressed week, temporary and part-time working, job sharing and home sharing. It is a work policy where employees can determine the exact number of hours they will work within a specific span of time.

Force-field Analysis: This analysis was developed by *Kurt Lewin*. It is suitable for individuals and is used by the manager who is planning the change, or as a means of stimulating thinking in a small group of people. It is a useful technique for looking at all the forces for and against a decision. In effect, it is a specialized method of weighing pros and cons. By carrying out this analysis you can plan to strengthen the forces supporting a decision, and reduce the impact of those opposing it.

a.

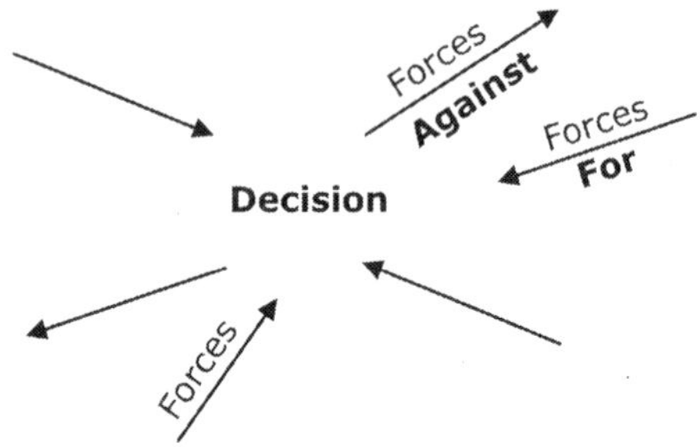

b.

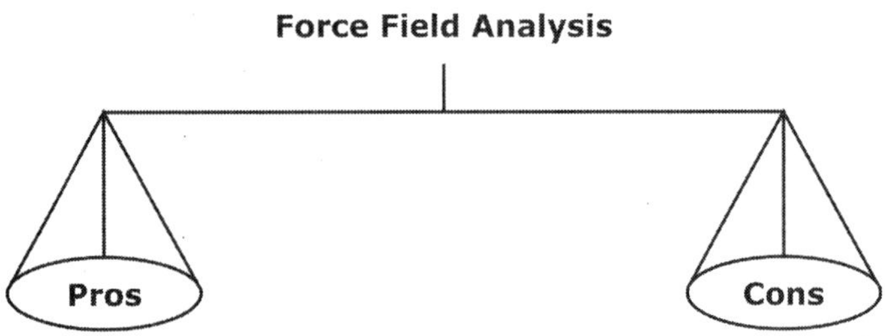

Forced Distribution: Forced distribution requires assessors to place a certain percentage of employees in each category.

Formal Group: A group is categorized as formal according to the degree to which the essential properties of the group are stated explicitly and formally, e.g. company board.

Formalization: It refers to the degree to which jobs within the organization are standardized by formulating and stating clear practices and procedures for carrying out work. It tries to standardize and regulate behaviour. It is an attempt to make relationships more visible and explicit.

Formal Organization: *Chester Barnard* defines it as a system of consciously coordinated activities of the two or more persons. It is a fixed set of rules of intra-organization procedures and structures which are usually set out in writing.

Forming: This is the initial stage of group formation marked by uncertainty and even confusion. Group members are not sure about the purpose, structure, task or leadership of the group. The group agrees on goals, discovers challenges and begins to tackle the task.

Frame-of-reference Training: It refers to the emphasis on consistency in the way different raters observe and evaluate an employee's behaviour and performance.

Free-agent HR Strategy: It is a strategy that combines emphasis on temporary employees with a focus on producing innovative goods and services.

Free Distribution: It refers to a method where the raters can put as many employees into each rating category.

FR (Forced Ranking): According to *Meisler* (2003), FR is a workforce management tool based on the premise that in order to develop and thrive, a corporation must identify its best and worst performers, then nurture the former and rehabilitate and discard the latter.

Meisler says, "It is an elixir that in these slow growth times has proved irresistible to scores of desperate corporate chieftains, but indigestible to a good many employees."

It is a performance intervention where the appraisers are required to rate the appraised ones according to a pre-specified criterion on which performance ranking would depend. It is a rating style where the raters make comparisons among employees.

Frustration: It occurs when one's strivings are thwarted, either by obstacles that block progress toward a desired goal or by absence of an appropriate goal. It may arise from internal or outer sources.

Functional Analysis of the Behaviour: It identifies both the antecedents (A) and consequences (C) of the target behaviour (B). It is, therefore, also known as an A-B-C analysis. A-B-C Analysis means:

- **A**ntecedent — The stimulus or stimuli to which an individual responds.
- **B**ehaviour — The behaviour that we see exhibited by an individual.
- **C**onsequence — The stimulus that an individual receives as a result of his/her behaviour.

There are two tools that can be used to help determine the motivation behind a particular behaviour:

- A functional behaviour **assessment** is a precise description of a behaviour, its context, and its consequences, with the intention of better understanding of the behaviour and those factors influencing it.
- A functional behaviour **analysis** begins as an assessment. However, it includes an added step of systematically altering the antecedents and checking the consequences of the behaviour to determine precisely which are the driving forces behind that behaviour.

Functional Authority: It is the right to detect or control specific activities that are under the span of control of other managers.

Functional Conflict: It refers to the conflict that is beneficial to organizational goals and objectives.

Functional Expert Role: It provides technical expertise related to hiring, training and compensating employees.

Functional Group: A group that gets things done and is held together by a common objective.

Functional Managers: They are responsible for different functions of an organization, such as production, marketing, finance, accounting and human resources.

Fundamental Attribution Error: It is a perception problem in which an individual is likely to attribute the behaviour of others to internal rather than external causes.

G

$$\textbf{Gain Per Employee} = \frac{\text{Operating gain}}{\text{Number of employees on full – time baiss}}$$

Gainsharing: Gainsharing is when an employer figures out how much to pay an employee based on how much money the company makes because of the employee's work. It may also take into account how much money the employee saves the company through changing processes or suppliers. In other words, it refers to the incentive programme that rewards the group for performing well jointly and thus reducing the costs.

Games Analysis: *Berne* codified socially dysfunctional behaviour patterns in terms of the games that people play.

GAS (General Adaptation Syndrome): *Hans Selye* coined this term as the body's response to stressors. It consists of three stages:

- Stage of alarm reaction
- Stage of resistance
- Stage of exhaustion

Gender Egalitarian: It refers to the equal opportunities for men and women. Sweden and Denmark score high on this dimension.

Gender Issues: These issues encompass the following concepts:

- The way infants are treated.
- Patterns for boys and girls.
- Socialization norms.
- Working of the educational system.

- Relationship of dating and married couples.
- Role behaviour in families.
- Job prescriptions.
- Working conditions and interactions between men and women in all areas of society.

Geocentric Approach: It refers to staffing key positions with the best people for the job regardless of their nationality.

Gestures: These are the signs used to convey specific meanings, e.g. shrugging your shoulders means, "I don't know." It is a form of non-verbal communication used instead of or in combination with verbal communication.

Glass border: It is the unseen but strong discriminatory barrier that blocks many women from opportunities for international assignments.

Glass ceiling: The term glass ceiling refers to situations where the advancement of a qualified person within the hierarchy of an organization is stopped at a lower level because of some form of discrimination. For example, a woman who is qualified for promotions to senior management level is overlooked because of subtle unspoken and unintended discrimination.

Global Corporation: It refers to a firm that has integrated worldwide operations through a centralized home office.

Global Expansion Strategy: It refers to the competitive business strategy which focuses upon raising the organization's presence in overseas markets.

Globalization: It is a trend towards a unified global economy where national borders mean relatively little. On the one hand, it creates new markets, wealth and new ventures; but on the other hand, it also gives rise to suffering, disorder and unrest. It is a force that touches the lives of all living across the globe leading to political, economic and cultural convergence.

Goal Commitment: It refers to the degree to which people dedicate themselves to achieve a goal.

Golden Handcuffs: These are the rewards and penalties designed to discourage key employees from leaving a company. The golden handcuff method is used when the employers want the employees, who may be tempted to leave, to stay with the company and make it worth their while to stay by putting significant benefits in their middle-term future.

Goal Planning: Developing a course of action that moves the organization toward accomplishing of general or specific goals.

Goal-setting Theory: It is a motivation theory that propounds that difficult and specific goals increase human performance because they affect efforts, persistence and direction of behaviour.

Goal Specificity: It refers to the performance goals which are clearly stated, explicit in their meaning and specific in terms of quantity or quality of performance.

Graphical Presentation: Graphical presentation of data is a useful aid in the analysis of data obtained from the pictorial treatment of frequency distribution.

Graphology: It can be defined as the scientific study of the social structure or personality of a human being through his/her writing. Graphology takes into consideration the size and slant of letters, word spacing, line spacing, margins and pressure applied on writing the words.

Great Man Theory of Leadership: It is a theory of leadership which states that leaders are born and not made. This theory believes that there are traits which the leader possesses and which make the leader effective. Some of these traits are intelligence, sociability, etc.

Grid Analysis/Decision Matrix Analysis: It is a useful technique for making a decision in corporates and in daily life situations. It is particularly powerful where a number of good alternatives are present and many different factors to be taken into account. This makes it a great technique to use in almost any important decision where there isn't a clear and obvious preferred option. Grid analysis creates a situation when one can take decisions confidently and rationally, while other group members are struggling to make a decision. This technique is often displayed on pamphlets, say, for electronic items when one brand tries to display its features and show its effectiveness over other brands.

$$\textbf{Grievance Handling Time} = \frac{\text{Number of days of grievance}}{\text{Total number of grievance cases}}$$

Grievance Procedure: It allows employees to make an appeal beyond their immediate manager.

Group: A group exists, when its members should:

- Feel motivated to join.
- Perceive the group as a unified unit of interacting people.
- Contribute in various amounts to the group processes.
- Have agreements and disagreements through various forms of interaction.

Group Dynamics: These describe how a group should be organized and conducted. These refer to the study of groups and group processes.

Group Goals: These goals represent the collective commitment that guides the performance of a group as a unitary system.

Group Think: It is a term coined by social psychologist *Irving Janis* in 1972. He defines it as deterioration of mental efficiency, reality testing and moral judgment that results from in-group pressures. It is a faulty decision-making in a group that occurs when there is high group cohesiveness and the group members experience the pressure to make a quality decision. It comes about when the group members try to minimize conflict, often ignoring the viewpoints outside the domain of consensus without critically examining, analyzing and evaluating ideas.

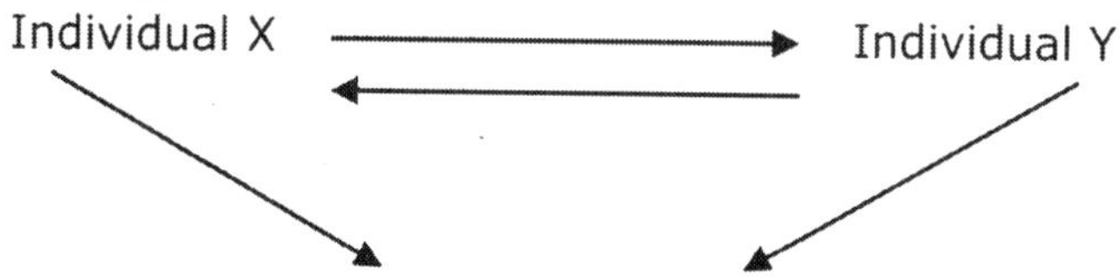

Common attitudes and values:

- Religion
- Marriage
- Lifestyle
- Politics
- Work
- Authority

Growth: Growth relates to increase in sales/revenue as well as associates and managers.

Growth Needs: These are concerned with the individual's intrinsic desire for personal development. They encompass cognitive, aesthetic and self-actualization needs.

- Cognitive need is the need to increase knowledge. Further, it is a need to learn, explore, discover and know about the world.
- Aesthetic needs are based on *Maslow's* beliefs. According to him, the humans always need something new and aesthetically pleasing to continue their journey towards self-actualization. Humans need to refresh themselves in the presence of beautiful nature while carefully observing and absorbing their surroundings to extract the beauty that the world has to offer.
- Self-actualization needs are those needs that aim for making the most of one's abilities.

Growth Strategy: It refers to the competitive business strategy which focuses on expansion of outputs of an organization in terms of its products and services into new markets.

GSI (Guest Satisfaction Index): It is a composite index of guest satisfaction based on four approaches to evaluate service quality:

- Guest satisfaction survey.
- An operations survey report.
- Guest comment cards.
- Unsolicited guest letters and telephone calls.

Guidance: *Henix Erickson* defines guidance as helping the students to become adjusted to their present situation and to plan their future in accordance with their interests, abilities and social needs.

H

Halo Effect: It is a perception problem in which an individual assesses a person positively or negatively in all situations based on an existing general assessment of the person.

Halo Error: It refers to the error related to rating which occurs when a holistic impression of the employee influences ratings rather than the performance of the employee.

Hawthorne Studies: *Hawthorne's* studies are generally recognized to be the beginning of the systematic study and understanding of organizational behaviour.

Health Hazards: They occur when a person comes in contact with hazardous situations which in turn cause injury or sickness.

Hedonistic View of Motivation: It refers to seek goals which give us good emotional feelings and to avoid those resulting in displeasure. In other words, pain or pleasure motivates us.

Herzberg Model of Enrichment: *Herzberg* gave this model in 1974. It is also known as Orthodox Job Enrichment (OJE). It constitutes six forms of enrichment:

- Accountability
- Achievement
- Feedback
- Workplace
- Control over resources
- Personal growth and development

Herzberg's approach has little to say about when and why the failures can be expected to occur.

Herzberg's Two Factor Theory: *Federick Herzberg* was a clinical psychologist and pioneer of management and motivational theory. The two factors in his theory include job satisfiers and job dissatisfiers. Job satisfiers are related to job content and job dissatisfiers are allied to job context. Satisfiers are motivators and dissatisfiers are hygiene factors. Herzberg's hygiene needs or maintenance factors in the workplace are:

- Policy
- Relationship with supervisor
- Work conditions
- Salary
- Company car
- Status
- Security
- Relationship with subordinates
- Personal life

Herzberg's research identified that true motivators were completely different factors. They are:

- Achievement
- Recognition
- Work itself
- Responsibility
- Advancement
- Personal growth

Heuristics: These are strategies, based on our past experience with problems, that are likely to lead to a solution but do not guarantee success.

High Context Culture: It is a type of culture where relationships are based on mutual trust and personal equations.

High Involvement Management: It is an approach that involves carefully selecting and training associates and giving them significant decision making power, information and incentive compensation.

High Need for Achievement (High N-Ach): People like to work in situations in which they have some control over the outcome because they are not gamblers. Those with high N-Ach tend to choose moderately difficult tasks feeling that they are challenging but within reach.

Histogram: It is plotted on exact limits. Histogram is preferred for ungrouped data. The horizontal top of each rectangle in a histogram is responsive to what occurs in one class-interval.

Home Sharing: It is working from home. Home working allows individuals to work at home utilizing computer-based technology to communicate with other people. In home working, the employee is able to balance with other commitments.

Horizontal Communication: The communication that takes place between associates at the same level.

Horizontal Specialization: It is an approach to jobs that creates many low skill level, short time cycle and reputative positions. Horizontal specialization usually occurs because growth in an organization requires additional management coordination and control.

Horizontal Team: A team where people from different departments are at the same hierarchical level.

Horns Effect Error: It refers to a single undesirable trait overshadowing many performance elements.

Host Country Nationals: It refers to the citizens of the country of foreign operation.

HR Accounting: The application of accounting principles, concepts and practical application in the evaluation and management of human assets.

$$\textbf{HR Budget} = \frac{\text{Total HR department budget}}{\text{Total sales of the company}} \times 100\%$$

$$\textbf{HR Staff Over Total Staff} = \frac{\text{Total HR employees}}{\text{Total number of employees}} \times 100\%$$

HRD (Human Resource Development): It is a term used to describe an integrated and holistic approach to changing work-related behaviour using a range of techniques and strategies. It is a human resource function concerned with equipping the employees with new knowledge and skills.

HRIS (Human Resource Information System): It is a management software used for data tracing which facilitates human resource planning, payroll and performance management. It refers to the systems and processes at the intersection of Human Resource Management (HRM) and Information Technology (IT). It is a comprehensive approach to acquire, store, analyse and control the flow of information throughout an organization.

HRP (Human Resource Planning): It is getting the right kind of people into the right jobs at the right time. It involves a process of forecasting the numbers and types of employees that will be needed in the future.

Human Capital: It is the sum of the skills, knowledge and general attributes of the people in an organization.

Human Capital Imitability: It refers to the extent to which the skills and talents of an organization's people can be copied by the other organization.

Human Capital Rareness: It refers to the extent to which the skills and talents of the people of an organization are unique in the industry.

Human Capital Value: It refers to the extent to which individuals are capable of producing work that supports an organization's strategy for competing in the market place.

Human Relations Movement: This movement originated in Hawthorne studies during the 1920s, which examined the group behaviour in workplace groups.

Human Resource Management (HRM) : It is the strategic and coherent approach to the management of an organization's most valued asset — the people working there who individually and collectively contribute to the achievement of the objectives of the business. It is a specialized field which studies people in organizations. It states principles which are in practice to study people in organizations.

Human Skills: These refer to the ability to work with and understand others, and to lead, motivate, reduce conflict and building group effort.

Human Resource Strategy: It is a strategy that focuses on different ways of managing employees of an organization.

Human Capital Developer Role: It is concerned with learning knowledge and developing skill.

Hybrid Control System: The hybrid control system refers to the controls prior to, during and after the performance of a work activity.

Hybrid Departmentalization: It refers to the grouping of organizational activities by two or more forms of departmentalization.

Hybrid Planning: It refers to both the domain and goal planning.

Hygiene Factors: These are the factors which do not give positive satisfaction although dissatisfaction results from their absence. These are extrinsic to the work itself, and include aspects such as company policies, supervisory practices or wages/salary.

Hypothesis: It is defined as a suggested answer to a problem.

I

Ice Breakers: These refer to an effective way of starting training sessions or team-building events. The interactive and often fun sessions are designed to take place before the main proceedings. These sessions help people get to know each other and bring into focus the purpose of the event. If an ice breaker session is well-designed and well-facilitated, it can really help get things off to a great start.

Idealistic Messaging: It refers to messaging positive information to potential employees.

IHRM (International Human Resource Management): It is a field that encompasses traditional functions of HR while simultaneously adapting to various environments around the world.

Imitation Strategy: It refers to a strategy that seeks to move into new markets only after their viability has already been proved.

Immutable Characteristics: These refer to individual characteristics that cannot be changed. These characteristics are race, sex, etc.

Impact Analysis/Change-Impact Analysis: It is also known as Impact-Change Analysis and Solution-Effect Analysis. This technique helps to think through the full impact of a proposed change. It is an essential part of the evaluation process for major decisions.

Implementer: An implementer is a hard worker who takes practical and efficient action.

Implicit Personality Theory: It is the tendency to define personality traits of people because they share certain characteristics with others.

Impression Management: It is the process by which people attempt to manage or control the perceptions which others form of them. It is the goal-directed activity of controlling or regulating information in order to influence the impressions formed by people who act as audience.

Incentive: Incentive is any financial or non-financial aid that provides motive toward a particular course of action. It is the additional pay which is above and beyond the basic salary, awarded to an employee.

Individualism: It is the degree to which members of society are comfortable focusing on personal goals and being rewarded for personal efforts and outcomes.

Individualistic Cultures: The managers tend to be more mobile, going from job to job. In this scenario, there is liberty for personal expression, independent thinking and personal choice.

Induction: It refers to an employee orientation programme which covers the company's history, job description, benefits, work culture and all the areas relevant for the employee to know about the organization. The orientation program may be the last phase of the recruitment process or the first phase of training. It enables the new recruits to get familiarized with new position description and their new organization.

Inductive Approach: In this approach, the job analyst begins by noting the characteristics of a job as the job is actually done in the organization. By careful examination of these job activities the analyst is able to produce summary statements in the form of job description describing what the typical worker in a given job actually does, which is then refined into statements of job specifications as to what the worker in a given job ought to do and finally job requirements relating the personal characteristics, abilities, skills, knowledge and training to perform the specified tasks.

Industrial Relations: It denotes a specialist area of organizational management and study. It is concerned with a particular set of phenomena associated with regulating the human activity of employment. It talks about relationship between management and workers comprising union activities.

Industrial/Vocational Trainees: Such trainees are those people who are recruited from approved and recognized institutes for a fixed time period normally not exceeding six months.

Inferential Statistics: Inferential statistics is concerned with an attempt to search for a general principle to be applied to a much larger domain beyond a group of individuals actually observed. Inferences are drawn from a study of sample about the conditions that exist in a population.

Influence: It refers to the ability to produce change in one's environment.

Informal Leader: An informal leader is a person whom the members of the group acknowledge as their leader irrespective of his rank or official position. Informal leader exists because the group members accept him/her as their leader.

Informational Social Influence: It was a concept given by *Deutsch and Gerard* (1955). It states that the group standards may provide information and guidance to an individual with respect to matters he cannot handle independently. One may act like others in a group simply because he is uncertain as to how he should otherwise behave.

Information Technology: It is a system where tools are based on silicon technology, designed to maintain data and documents, and provide analysis that support employers and employees of an organization.

Ingratiating Tactics: Such tactics are used to get you in a good mood or to think favourably of the influence agent before asking you to do something.

Initiating Structure: It is the job of a task-oriented leader who focuses on attainment of tasks, objectives, solving problems and maintaining processes.

Injunctive Norms: Injunctive norms are the ones which people feel are correctly based on beliefs and morals. These norms specify what ought to be done, i.e. what is approved or disapproved behaviour in a given situation.

Inn: A place, smaller in size, with modest board and lodging facilities.

Innovation Strategy: It is a strategy that emphasizes the introduction of major new products and services.

Inspirational Appeal: It refers to making an emotional request or proposal that arouses enthusiasm by appealing to your values and ideas or by increasing your confidence that you can do it.

Instinct: Our natural basic need for our survival. It is unlearned, fixed inherited disposition towards a specific behaviour.

Intangible Assets: Intangible assets refer to non-physical assets that represent value to an organization. They are not tangible as they cannot be seen or counted.

Integration: It refers to the efforts of an organization to integrate different work units.

Integrative Bargaining: It refers to the process where individuals are trying to make more of something. It is usually explained in terms of a pie. It is also referred as zero-sum or win-lose bargaining.

Intellectualization: It is a mental process in which the intensity of the anxiety is reduced by a retreat into detached, unemotional, abstract language.

Intelligence: It is an aggregate global capacity to think rationally, to deal effectively and to adjust in one's environment, according to *Wechsler*.

Intensity: The intensity principle of attention states that the more intense the external stimulus the more likely it is to be perceived.

Interaction Orientation: It refers to an aptitude to interact with others, i.e. having a happy time with others.

Interest Rate Risk: The interest rates affect the success of projects. They directly affect the net present value or the real rate of return on investments in projects.

Inter-group Relations: The social psychology terms these relations as the behaviour of different social groups towards each other which are at the same time separate and unavoidably shackled together (in the sense that the fate of each of them depends to a large extent upon the nature of its relations with the others). These relations are seen as a joint function of certain social psychological processes and of the structure of the objective relations between the groups.

Internal Consistency Method of Reliability: It is different from other methods of reliability. Reliability of a test through this method is based on a number of items in the test and the average correlation among test items.

Internal Environment: It refers to organization norms, culture, climate, equipments and management practices.

Internal Equity: Internal equity is the perception of the employees about fairness based on how much they are paid relative to others working in the same organization.

International Ethics: These refer to a code of conduct focused on corruption, exploitation of labour and environment impact.

Internal Labour Orientation: It is a perspective that focuses on hiring the people at a younger age and then retaining them for long periods in the same organization.

Internal Locus of Control: The internal locus of control refers to the individuals who believe that their behaviour is governed by personal actions and effort. It is a belief system of individuals that their skills and abilities are the primary determinants of their destinies. This concept was given by *Julian Rotter* (1966) but later developed by *Zimbardo* (1985).

Internal Sourcing: It is a recruiting strategy that recruits people by transferring them to job openings. In other words, various job openings are filled by people who are already working in the organization.

International Corporation: It refers to a domestic firm that uses its existing capabilities to move into overseas markets.

Inter-role Distance: It arises when an individual occupies more than one role and there is a conflict between the two roles.

Interval Scale: This scale includes categories which are mutually exclusive, exhaustive and arranged in order of magnitude at equal intervals.

Intra-role Conflict: It arises when an individual develops expectation as a result of socialization and identification with significant others.

Intrinsic Motivation: Intrinsic motivation is in contrast with extrinsic motivation. Intrinsic motivation will make people to do a job for fun. It is a far stronger motivator than extrinsic motivation. These are the people who carry passion to their work desk. It refers to the joyful state of the organism. In other words, it is the motivation that comes from within the individual rather from any external source such as recognition or monetary benefits.

Intrinsic Rewards: Intrinsic rewards stem from personal satisfaction derived from a job well done.

Involuntary Absenteeism: It occurs when an employee absents himself out of sickness or factors out of the reach of the individual.

Involuntary Turnover: It is a situation where the employer chooses to terminate the services of employees.

$$\textbf{Involuntary Turnover Rate} = \frac{\text{Number of layoffs} + \text{retirements} + \text{disability} + \text{dismissals}}{\text{Total number of employees in specific period}}$$

ISB (Incomplete Sentence Blank): It is used in selection of personnel in industries. It is a semi-structured projective device. It assesses the subject's level of adjustments.

$$\textbf{IT Staff Over Total Staff} = \frac{\text{Total number of IT empolyees}}{\text{Total number of employees}} \times 100\%$$

J

JCM (Job Characteristic Model): It is a motivational job design where the work has activities which are in turn enjoyed by employees.

Job: It a single position or a group of similar positions in one establishment in which the work activities and objectives are similar in terms of actions, methodologies, materials, products, and for workers characteristics and in which the array of work activities differ significantly from those of other positions. In general, job is a collection of activities that are performed at work.

Job Analysis: It is the process of developing job-related information and it can serve as the cornerstone of an integrated human resource programme.

Job Appointing Letter: It is an HR document which has details such as joining date, salary along with some allowances, job descriptions and reporting hierarchical level.

Job-based Fit: It refers to matching the employee's expertise with the tasks associated with a particular job.

Job-based Pay: It is the payment to an employee based upon the tasks performed in his/her work domain.

Job Content Decision: It refers to the inherent nature of work.

Job Context Decision: It refers to the factors that surround the job and are not part of one's job.

Job Description: It is a written summary describing a particular job classification or position. It is about what is to be done at work.

Job Design: It is an important application area for work motivation and the study of organizational behaviour. Through job design, stress can be reduced, motivation can be enhanced, satisfaction of the employee can be increased and performance can be improved.

Job Engineering: It is concerned with product, process and tool design; plant layout; standard operating procedures; work measurement and standards; worker methods and human machine interactions.

Job Enlargement: It is the act of increasing in size or volume or quantity or scope.

Job Enrichment: It is the act of making the job fuller, more meaningful and rewarding by making changes in challenges in the employee's present work. It can be addition or withdrawal of challenges. Job enrichment can occur if the employee is promoted, demoted, and on transfer of job and job rotation.

Job Involvement: It refers to the psychological involvement with a particular job.

Job Performance: It refers to the performance of a job, relative to one's expectation of the performance of that job. In general, it is the contribution that individuals give to the organization where they are employed.

Job Posting System: It refers to a system in which the organization announces job openings to all employees on a bulletin board or a company newsletter or through a phone recording or computer system.

Job Redesign: It is the process of reassessing task groupings to create a new set of activities that an employee has to do in specific situations.

Job Rotation: It involves the process of combining two or more simplified jobs into a pattern of work rotation. It is a lateral work assignment which is time-bound and with a purpose of helping employees to develop new skills and knowledge.

Job Satisfaction: It can be termed as a pleasurable or positive emotional state resulting from the appraisal of one's job or job experience.

Job-sharing: It means that two part-time employees share the same full-time job.

Job-sharing: It allows two or more people to share a specific job by agreement taking a proportion each.

Job Specification: It defines the education, training, qualifications, experience and competencies required by the employer in the employee.

Johari Window: It is a very popular descriptive framework for analyzing the dynamics of interpersonal behaviour. It was developed by *Joseph Luft* and *Harry Ingham*.

Judgemental Decision-making Approach: It refers to the majority approval or disapproval by a group of experts.

Jungle Fighter: It refers to an individual with lust for power. He/she experiences life and work in a jungle where "eat or be eaten" is the rule and the winners destroy the losers. It implies survival of the fittest.

K

Knowledge: Knowledge refers to the facts and principles and their awareness.

Knowledge Management: It is a concept in which an enterprise deliberately and comprehensively gathers, organizes, shares and analyzes its knowledge in terms of its resources and HR policies. It is the source which translates ideas into business value. It is a process of acquiring, innovating, assimilating, coordinating and using information and experiences to achieve organizational objectives.

Knowledge of Results: This psychological state involves the degree to which employees understand how they are performing in the job.

KPI (Key Performance Indicators): These define the basis for measuring the performance of an employee.

L

Lab Experiments: The purpose of lab experiments is to discover under pure conditions relationship between dependent and independent variables and how variation in one is invariably followed by variation in the other.

Laboratory Training: It provides the participants with an intensive experience of sharing, participation and change through carefully designed exercises and training events, important to the participants and relevant to the programme.

Labour Force Trends: They are the trends concerning the number and types of people who are employed or searching for jobs.

Labour Relations: These refer to the interactions between the employer or the management and the employees of the organization.

Labour Union: It refers to the organization representing the collective interests of the workers.

Law of Effect: It is a principle of psychology described by *Edward Thorndike* in 1898. The law holds that responses to stimuli that produce a satisfying or pleasant state of affairs in a particular situation are more likely to occur again in the situation. Conversely, responses that produce a discomforting, annoying or unpleasant effect are less likely to occur again in the situation.

Layoffs: It refers to a large number of terminations of services of employees from the organization that is unrelated to their performance.

Layoff Survivors: Those employees who continue their services in the organization even when their coworkers are laid off.

Layoff Victims: These are the individuals who are the victims of layoff.

Leader: According to *Sharter and Stogdill*, whosoever occupies leader's office is a leader.

Leader-Member Exchange Model: *Graen* and *Schliemann* (1978) emphasize that the relationship between each leader-subordinate pair must be considered separately because leaders behave differently with each subordinate. This theory is also known as Vertical Dyadic Linkage Theory.

Leading: It includes motivating employees, directing others, selecting the most effective communication channels and resolving conflicts.

Learning: It is a process through which individuals undergo permanent change in their knowledge, skill and attitude based on their experience while dealing with their environment.

Learning Organization: *Chris Argyris* and his colleagues coined this term and defined the distinction between first order or single-loop and second order or double-loop learning.

- *Single-loop learning*: It involves improving the organization's capacity to achieve known objectives. It is associated with routine and behavioural learning.

It means the organization is learning without significant change in its basic assumptions.

- *Double-loop learning*: It re-evaluates the nature of the organization's objectives and the values and beliefs surrounding them. This type of learning involves changing the organization's culture.

Leave Vacancy Employee: An individual who is engaged in place of a permanent employee or probationer who is temporarily absent.

Legitimate Power: This power source was identified by *French* and *Raven*. It stems from the internalized values of the other individuals that give the legitimate right to the agent to influence them.

Life Insurance: It is a form of compensation made to the family members of the deceased insured person.

Line: It carries command or decision making responsibilities over subordinates.

Lockout : It refers to the situation where the employers close down the workplace as a result of labour dispute.

Locus of Control: It refers to the extent to which an individual attributes control of events to self and environment. This concept was given by *Julian Rotter* in 1966 and later developed by *Zimbardo*, 1985.

Logical Error: It refers to the perception error in which an individual forms an impression of a person on the basis of only one or two central characteristics.

Longitudinal Method: In this method same individuals are observed at different points in time.

Long-term Specialists: These candidates are hired for long periods within the organization and they help in developing specific expertise.

Loyal Soldier HR Strategy: It is a strategy that combines emphasis on permanent employees with a focus on reducing costs.

M

Mail Questionnaire: It is used for marketing purposes. It is a very simple and emotional method, but there is no guarantee about the return of questionnaire.

Majority-wins Scheme: The group arrives at the decision that was initially supported by the majority.

Maintenance: It is the third stage of career development which involves optimizing talents or capabilities.

Maintenance Synergy: It refers to energy expended to maintain the group and to sustain the attraction of individual members to remain in the group.

Management Development: It refers to a systematic programme which helps employees (same organization or different organization) gain and apply knowledge, skills, insights and attitudes to manage work efficiently.

Management Grid: It was given by *Blake* and *Mouton*. It proposes various leadership styles based on degrees of combination between concern for people and concern for production.

Management Teams: These teams consist of senior level managers who coordinate their respective teams.

(MT) Management Trainees: They are usually taken up by the organization after signing a memorandum of agreement.

Management Training: It is an organizational development intervention designed to increase the self awareness of individuals and their sensitivity towards other people.

Managers: They are individuals who achieve goals through other people.

Managing Diversity: It refers to enabling employees to perform to their maximum potential by changing the culture and infrastructure of the organization.

$$\textbf{Marketing Staff over Total Staff} = \frac{\text{Number of marketing employees}}{\text{Total number of employees}} \times 100\%$$

Market Risk: It refers to changes in the price level of products in the market and reflects a fundamental interplay between the forces of supply and demand which are not transparent. Accurate timing is the critical factor in this game.

Masculinity: *Hofstede* defines it as the extent to which the dominant values of a society emphasize assertiveness and the acquisition of money and other material things.

Maslow's Theory: It states that motivational needs could be arranged in a hierarchical manner.

Matrix: It is a structure that creates dual lines of authority and combines functional and product departmentalization. The strength of the matrix lies in its ability to facilitate coordination among multiple complex and interdependent activities of the organization. The direct and frequent contact between different specialities in the matrix can make communication all the more flexible.

Matrix Organization: It is a project organization plus a functional organization. In other words, when a project structure is superimposed on a functional structure, the result is a matrix.

MBO (Management by Objectives): It is a management process which focuses on negotiation of task objectives or KRAs which are then responsible for the fulfilment of objectives.

Mean: It is an arithmetic average of the individual scores. It is the sum of the separate scores divided by their number.

Meaningfulness: This cognitive state involves the degree to which employees perceive their work as being important and valuable and making a valued contribution.

Measurement: It is the process of assigning numbers to observations.

Measures of Central Tendency: These represent the central value for a group of individuals. The term 'average' stands for any measure of central tendency. The three averages or measures of central tendency are: mean, median and mode.

Measures of Variability: These measures express quantitatively the extent to which the scores in a set scatter about or cluster together.

Mechanistic Organization: It has tight control, extensive work specialization, high formalization and high centralization.

Median: A median is defined as the mid-point of a distribution — 50% cases lie below the median and the other 50% lie above it.

Mediation: Mediation is the process under which a third party intervenes to resolve a dispute among the employees or between the management and the employees. This process is more informal than arbitration. There are no witnesses nor any cross-examination unlike court proceedings.

Membership Group: It is a group to which an individual belongs formally in name or body, e.g. alumni associations.

Mental Disabilities: The mental impairment that limits an individual's ability to lead a normal life.

Mentor: A trusted counsellor, coach or advisor who provides advice and assistance. According to *Hunt* and *Michael* (1983), mentors are those individuals with advanced experience and knowledge who are committed to providing upward mobility and support for their protégé's careers.

Merit-based System: It is a performance management system that particularly seeks to identify and recognize the inputs of employees with superior performance.

Merit Bonus: It refers to one-time payment to an employee which is based upon good performance. It can be quarterly, annually or half-yearly depending upon the increment policy of the organization.

Merit Pay Increase: It refers to an increase in salary or basic remuneration given to the employee depending upon his/her level of performance.

Message: It is the stimulus which the source transmits to the receiver. It is composed of symbols designed to convey the intended meaning.

Mid-career Plateau: It is a stage where an employee is no longer receiving promotion or advancement opportunities in the organization, and more challenging job assignments are also less frequent.

Mission Statement: It is a precise description of what an organization proposes to do for its clients and employees.

MNC (Multinational Corporation): It refers to a firm with independent business units operating in multiple countries.

Mode: It has been defined as the single score which occurs with maximum frequency in the distribution.

Model: A model is an abstraction of reality, a simplified representation of some real-world phenomenon.

Modern Racism: It refers to a subtle form of discrimination that occurs despite people knowing that it is wrong to be prejudiced against other racial groups and their perception that they believe themselves are not racists.

Monitor-Evaluator: The monitor-evaluators are good at seeing all the options. They have a strategic perspective and can judge situations accurately. They can be overcritical and are not usually good at provoking and encouraging others.

Monochronic Time Orientation: It refers to doing only one task in a given time period.

Monolithic Organization: It refers to an organization which is demographically and culturally homogeneous.

Monte Carlo Analysis: This analysis helps in bringing uncertainty and risk into forecasting.

Moonlighting: It is defined as an employee doing an additional job which is different from his/her routine job. Working part-time or on hourly basis also comes under this.

Motel: This term is derived from the phrase "motor hotels". These are the rest houses found on the highways. They are used by the travellers who go on long journeys by road. Their length of stay is usually overnight.

Motion: People will pay more attention to moving objects in their field of vision than to stationary objects.

Motivation: It refers to the driving and pulling forces which result in a persistent behaviour directed toward a particular goal. It is a process that starts with a physiological or psychological deficiency or need that activates a behaviour or a drive that is aimed at a goal or incentive. It can be traced to Latin word "movere" which means "to move".

Motivational Interviewing: It is defined as a client-centred, directive method for enhancing intrinsic motivation to change by exploring and resolving ambivalence.

MPS (Motivating Potential Score):

$$= \frac{[\text{Skill variety} + \text{Task identity} + \text{Task significance}]}{3} \times \text{Autonomy} \times \text{Feedback}$$

$$\text{MPS} = \frac{[\text{SV} + \text{TI} + \text{TS}]}{3} \times \text{A} \times \text{F}$$

MTOP (Management Training On Property): MTOPs are conducted locally for hotel's management staff. They are composed of approximately 20 training modules, geared for line managers with specific skills necessary to effectively manage their employees on a day-to-day basis. The different programs offered with MTOP include:

- Training the trainer
- Leadership
- Communication
- Time management
- Interview skill
- Problem solving
- Finance
- Effective meetings, etc.

Multicultural Organization: It is characterized by core cultural values and an ongoing commitment to eliminate social oppression throughout the organization.

Multi-unionism: It is used to describe the existence of more than a single union in relation to the collective bargaining structure. Two distinct forms of multi-unionism are:

- Type A — Where each distinct group in an organization or industry is organized and represented by a different union.
- Type B — Where there is more than one union competing to organize and represent a distinct group within the organization or industry.

Myth: A myth involves an element of truth, but it often gets distorted or exaggerated over a period of time.

N

N-Ach (Need for Achievement): This term was introduced by *David McClelland* referring to an individual's desire for significant accomplishment, mastering of skills, control or high standards. N-Ach is related to the difficulty of tasks people choose to undertake.

Narrative: It is used to refer to structures of knowledge and storied ways of knowing.

Narrative Analysis: It can be used for systematic interpretation of other's interpretations of events.

Narrative Rating: It refers to a rating style where the rater writes a paragraph about the employee's performance.

Need: It is an organic state of deficiency or excess.

Negative Feedback: The information that provides a description about aspects where the employees need training and improvement.

Negative Reinforcement: It strengthens and increases behaviour by the termination or withdrawal of an undesirable consequence.

Negotiation: *Neale* and *Bazerman* defined it as a decision making process among interdependent parties who do not share unidentical preferences. It is through negotiation that the parties decide what each would give and take in their relationships.

Networking: It refers to hiring, managing and restoring contacts for use in job situation for different purposes.

Network Organization: These are highly flexible and market-controlled mechanisms rather than administrative procedures. Firms with this new structure arrayed themselves on an industry value chain according to their core competencies, obtaining complementary resources through strategic alliances and outsourcing.

Neutral Culture: According to *Trompenaars*, in this culture, emotions are not outwardly expressed.

NGT (Nominal Group Technique): In NGT, a group of individuals addresses an issue. The issue is described to the group and each individual writes a list of ideas. No discussion among the numbers is permitted.

Nominal Scale: It includes variables which are mutually exclusive and exhaustive and are arranged in order of magnitude.

Non-governmental Organization (NGO): It is a legally constituted organization created by private organizations or people with no participation or representation of any government. The NGOs which are funded totally or partially by governments maintain their non-governmental status insofar as they exclude government representatives from membership in the organization.

Non-operational Goals: These move from time to time through a sequence of operational goals.

Non-programmed Decisions: The decisions which are poorly structured because information is ambiguous. There is no clear procedure for making the decision and the goals often are vague, according to *Simon* (1960).

Non-task Conflicts: These are disagreements and incompatibilities among group members about personal issues that are not task-related, but are based upon personality clash and interpersonal antagonism.

Non-verbal Communication: It refers to communication that takes place without using language, such as facial expressions or body language.

Normative Commitment: It involves the employee's feelings of obligation to stay with the organization. It is an internalized concept.

Normative Decision Theory: It was given by *Vroom* and *Yetton* (1973). This theory focuses on single aspect of leadership. It proposes five styles on a continuum of leader behaviour ranging from autocratic to complete participation.

Normative Social Influence: The group norms may be a key to the individual's acceptance by others in the group. He may adhere to group norms to gain some advantage like the reward of social acceptance. It is instrumental in achieving some personal goal.

Norming: In this stage, the members begin to settle into cooperation and collaboration. They have a feeling of belongingness with high cohesion, group identity and camaraderie.

Norms: These are the standards of behaviour including guidelines on how much work to do. In many organizations, norms come down to "do not do too much; do not do too little".

Novelty and Familiarity: It states that either a novel or a familiar external situation can serve as an attention-getter.

O

Obedience: It occurs when the authority figure commands focal person to obey.

Observational Learning/Imitation: It occurs when an individual models the other person's behaviour. It is learning that occurs as a function of observing, retaining and replicating a novel behaviour executed by others. There are four key processes of observational learning:

- Attention
- Retention
- Reproduction
- Motivation

Occupation: It refers to a group of somewhat related jobs in different organizations.

Occupational Health and Safety: It focuses upon employee's physical and mental well-being.

Occupational Interest Inventories: These are used to supplement tests of aptitude and those of intelligence. Several self-answering occupational preference questionnaires or inventories have been devised to provide information regarding an individual's interests in a variety of activities.

Occupational Outlook Handbook: It is a nationally recognized source which assists individuals to guide them in their career.

Occupational Union: *Bell* noted that this type of union seeks to unite all workers of a particular craft, trade, occupation or grade of skill, irrespective of the industry in which they happen to be engaged.

Ohio-State Leadership Studies: These studies were done by *Fleishman* (1973) and *Stogdill* (1974). These studies show that leaders' characteristic of initiating structure and consideration for others make them effective.

Ombudsperson: This concept provides an outlet for persons who have been treated unfairly or in a depersonalized manner by large, bureaucratic government or private organizations.

On-the-job Training: It refers to actual practice on the job.

Open Door Policy: It refers to a situation where the manager is easily accessible to every employee. It is a continuous invitation for employees to come and talk about anything that is troubling them. In other words, there is an open communication amongst employees and their relevant bosses.

Open-ended Questions: In these type of questions, the respondent is free to give any answer in a paragraph.

Operant Conditioning: It is concerned primarily with learning that occurs as a consequence of behaviour.

Operational Goals: These are likely to be somewhat more transitory and shorter in range.

Operational Plan: It is a short-term plan that outlines the implementation of a strategic plan during a specified operational period.

Operational Risk: It involves a 'catch all' for risk factors within an enterprise and is due to inadequate internal controls, human error or failure of IT systems.

Open Shop: An open shop is a place of employment where one is not required to join or financially support a labour union as a condition of hiring or continued employment.

Ordinal Scale: It includes variables which are mutually exclusive and exhaustive and also indicate the order of magnitude of some variables.

Organic Organization: It is characterized by loose structure, low specialization, low formalization and decentralization.

Organization: An organization is referred to as a collection of individuals, whose members may change over time, forming a coordinated system of specialized activities for the purpose of achieving certain goals over some extended period of time.

Organizational Behaviour: It refers to the study and application of the human side of management and organization.

(OBMod) Organizational Behaviour Modification: It has been developed and used by *Luthans* and *Kreitner* as a behavioural approach to the management of human resources for performance improvement.

Organizational Citizenship: It is the discretionary behaviour that is not part of an employee's formal job requirements but that nevertheless promotes the effective functioning of the organization.

Organizational Climate: This is an overall feeling that is conveyed by the physical layout, the way participants interact and the way members of the organization conduct themselves with customers or other outsiders.

Organizational Commitment: It is most often defined as:

- A strong desire to remain a member of a particular organization.
- A willingness to exert high levels of effort on behalf of the organization.
- A definite belief in and acceptance of the values and goals of the organization.

Organizational Culture: *Edgar Schein* defines it as a pattern of basic assumptions which are invented, discovered or developed by a given group as it learns to cope with its problems of external adaptation and internal integration, and this pattern has worked well enough to be considered valuable and therefore to be taught to new members as the correct way to perceive, think and fall in relation to those problems.

Organizational Effectiveness: It is regarded as a dependent variable, i.e. as an outcome of the organization's contextual, structural, strategic or process variables. It is also a systemic variable affected by these variables and in turn affecting them.

Organizational Inertia: It refers to the tendency to maintain the status quo.

Organizational Life Stages: They correspond to stages under which every organization goes through.

Organizational Nesting: It refers to organizations embedded within organizations.

Organizational Politics: It involves those activities undertaken within organizations to acquire, develop and use power and other resources to obtain one's preferred outcomes in a situation in which there is uncertainity or a lack of consensus about choices.

Organizational Psychology: It is referred to as organizational behaviour. It is concerned with issues that are molar in nature. It focuses on issues such as study and management of individual differences and diversity; motivation; leadership theories; communication process; dynamics of group behaviour; well being and malfunctional and dysfunctional behaviour at work and last but not the least organizational design, organization development and its culture.

Organizational Silence: It occurs when important information is not given to those who are important as they have the authority to act on it.

Organizational Structure: It refers to those features that determine the interaction patterns that link people to work. Organizational structure defines how job tasks are formally divided, grouped and coordinated

Organizational Theory: It tends to be more macro-oriented than organization behaviour and is concerned primarily with organization structure and design.

Organization-based Fit: It refers to matching the characteristics of employees to the organization culture.

Organization Development (OD): According to *French* and *Bell*, OD is a long range effort to improve an organization's problem-solving and renewal processes, particularly through a more effective and collaborative management of organization's formal work teams with the assistance of a change agent or catalyst, and the use of the theory and technology of applied behavioural science including action research.

Organization Size: The organizations employing 2,000 or more people tend to have more specialization, more departmentalization, more vertical levels and more rules and regulations than do small organizations. The impact of size becomes less important as an organization expands.

Organizing: It determines what tasks are to be done, who is to do them, how the tasks are to be grouped, who reports to whom, and where decisions are to be made.

Orientation Training: It is to acquaint new employees with the company.

Outcome or Goal Statement: This statement refers to goals that managers hope to attain.

Outcomes: These are attained after exchanging the individual's inputs.

Outsourcing: It became one of the important activities in the 1980s. It refers to non-core operations performed by an external agency specializing in the management of those operations. It refers to the practice of turning over an entire function (shipping, pay roll, benefits administration, security, computer networking) to an outside specialist.

Overtime: It is the work done in addition to regular working hours.

Overtime = Number of hours worked – Number of working hours

Owned and Accepted Goals: These are arrived at through participation. They seem preferable to assigned goals.

P

$$\textbf{P (IH)} = \frac{\text{Total number of positions filled from the organization}}{\text{Total job positions available}} \times 100\%$$

P(IH) Index assesses the likelihood of an employee being selected from the organization itself.

Package: It refers to a combination of benefits and wages that employees receive due to collective bargaining.

Paired Comparison Analysis: It is an analysis about different options and it helps to set priorities where there are conflicting demands over the resources. It helps to work out the importance of a number of options relative to each other. The results are tallied and the option having the highest score is the chosen option.

Panel Technique: The same set of persons are studied and restudied at regular intervals to study the opinions and growth and change of opinions of the subjects.

Paradigm: It comes from the Greek word *paradeigma* which translates as model, pattern or example.

Paralanguage: It refers to how something is said, such as tone of voice, pitch of voice and how silence is used.

Parallel Team: It refers to a team that performs functions which the main organization does not.

Parameter: An index that is descriptive of a particular thing.

Parent Country Nationals: The citizens of the home country of a multinational corporation.

Pareto Analysis: Pareto analysis is a formal technique for finding the changes that will give the biggest benefits. It is a very simple statistical technique that helps you choose the most effective changes to make. It is found to be effective where many possible courses of action are competing for attention. Pareto analysis not only shows the most important problem to solve, it also gives a score showing how severe the problem is. It uses the Pareto principle, i.e. by doing 20% of work you can generate 80% of the overall benefit of doing the entire job.

Parity-based System: A performance management system that seeks to recognize inputs of all employees without promoting some over others.

Participative Leadership: It occurs when the leader allows subordinates to participate in decisions that affect their work.

Particularism: According to *Trompenaars*, it is the belief that circumstances dictate how ideas and practices should be applied.

Path-Goal Theory: The Path-Goal Theory was developed by *Robert House* (1971). It is based on the Expectancy Theory of Motivation. The manager's job is viewed as guiding the workers to choose the best paths for reaching their goals. It focuses on the kinds of behaviour a leader must exercise to allow subordinates to achieve their goals.

PAQ (Position Analysis Questionnaire): It is a method of job analysis that uses a structured questionnaire to study task activities. It lists more worker-oriented job elements that can be used broadly. It was developed by *Mc. Cormick, Jeanert* and *Mecham*. It consists of 187 job elements in six divisions which yield 45 psychologically oriented factors. The six dimensions are:

- Information input
- Mental processes
- Work output
- Relationships with others
- Job context
- Other job characteristics

Pay Survey: It refers to gathering information about the pay packages offered in different organizations across the same industry often used to devise a benchmark strategy.

Pay without Work: It refers to the paid leaves.

PEM (Punctuated Equilibrium Model): In this model, the group development depends upon the fulfilment of task at hand and the deadlines for that task, not on linear stages.

Pension: It is a fixed sum of money that is paid to an individual who has retired and is entitled to receive the benefit under the pension plan.

Percentile Rank: These are derived scores. They describe the location of the raw score relative to other scores in the distribution. They are comparable, easy to comprehend and are relatively meaningful to persons having no statistical training.

Perception: It is a process by which individuals organize and assimilate meaning from the sensory stimuli received from the environment. It is a very complex cognitive process that yields a unique picture of the world, a picture that may be quite different from reality.

Perceptual Constancy: It refers to the tendency of animals and humans to see familiar objects as having standard shape, size, colour or location regardless of changes in the angle of perspective, distance or lighting. It gives a person a sense of stability in a changing world.

Performance: It is the outcome of organizational employees that meet organizational objectives.

Performance Appraisal: It is a process of recording and assessment of employee performance, potential and development. It is also known as pay evaluation, or merit rating efficiency audit as stated by IIM, Ahmedabad.

Performance Management: It refers to the process of assessing and providing feedback about an employee's inputs in the organization.

Performance Objective: It defines specific, individual objectives in the areas of project, processes, business as usual and core values for which the employee will be held accountable.

Performance Tests: These tests were developed to provide a means of testing individuals with language handicaps and blind persons with whom an adequate rating could not be obtained with such tests that depended largely on language, number and abstraction.

Performing: This is the stage where the group is fully functioning and devoted to effectively accomplishing the tasks.

Permanent Employee: A permanent employee is an individual who has been engaged on a regular basis. The term refers to any individual who has been confirmed in writing as a permanent employee either at the time of initial recruitment or after satisfactory completion of the stipulated probationary period applicable to him/her as per his/her employment terms in the same or any other occupation in the organization.

Person Analysis: It refers to the process that helps to identify the individuals who need training and which individual characteristics will influence the effectiveness of training.

Personal Accomplishment: It refers to the tendency to evaluate oneself critically, particularly with regard to one's work with clients.

Personal development: It refers to self-development and development of others. Self-development includes enhancing self-knowledge, self-esteem, developing talents, increasing one's employability, enhancing quality of life, maintaining work-life balance and in totality working towards self-actualization. The development of others refers to development and improvement of methods, programmes, techniques related to largely one's field. But this kind of development will turn to be a part of self-development.

Personal Frustration: It occurs from personal inadequacy.

Personality: According to *G. Allport,* the personality is the dynamic organization within the individual of those psychophysical systems that determine his characteristic behaviour and thought.

Personality Tests: These tests are used to evaluate and test non-intellectual traits of personality such as emotion, thinking patterns and behaviour. Growing interests in scientific and clinical study provided the stimulus for the development of personality tests. Personnel problems during World War I provided impetus for their growth as well.

Personnel Psychologists: Private and public organizations apply psychology to problems of management and employee training, to supervision of personnel, to improve communication within the organization, to counsel employees and to alleviate industrial strife. The applied psychologists who do this work are sometimes called personnel psychologists.

Personnel Testing: For such testing, ability tests and tests of specific skills are used. Ability tests are used for screening volunteers, placements of soldiers according to their skills or abilities, assess training needs, and success of training programmes. These are part of management development and career counselling programme.

PEST (Political, Economical, Social & Technological Analysis) : This model helps to identify the SWOT factors. It is used to assess the market from a specific standpoint. It can be presented in a matrix form and factors such as ecological, legislative and industry should be included within the matrix.

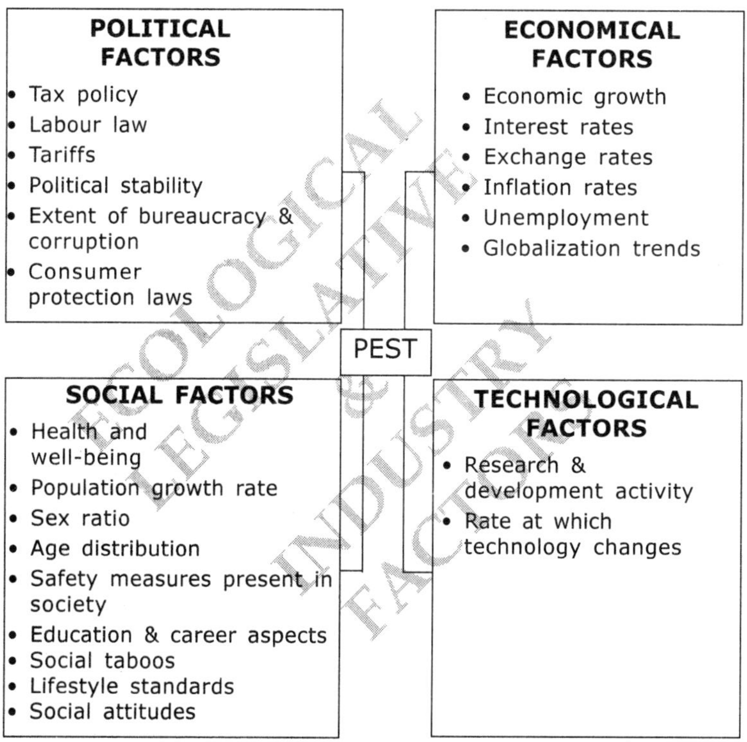

PEST Matrix

Philosophy: These are the policies that set forth the organization's beliefs about how employees and customers are to be treated.

Phronesis: It is knowledge which is the result of experience and social practice. It cannot be easily shared. It is personal and has profound meaning only for the individual who has lived the experience.

Physical Disability: The physical impairment that limits an individual's ability to lead a normal life.

Picketing: It is a tactic used by trade unions to dissuade others in a non-violent way from entering the work premises during a strike in order to stop any working activity. It is a protest where workers get together outside the workplace.

Piece Rate Incentive: It refers to certain amount of incentive paid for each piece of work.

Plan: It is a layout of any procedure to carry out.

Planning: It includes defining goals, establishing strategy and developing plans to coordinate activities.

Plant: It refers to the thoughtful innovator to provide creative ideas.

Plural Organization: It is an organization that has a diverse workforce and that ensures that employees are well treated. Diversity is tolerated but not fostered.

PMI (Plus Minus Interesting): PMI is an important decision making tool. It is a useful tool for weighing the pros and cons of a decision. When one course of action is chosen, PMI helps to check whether it is worth taking.

POB (Positive Organizational Behaviour): According to *Luthans* (2002), it is the study and application of positively-oriented human resource strengths and psychological capabilities that can be measured, developed and effectively managed for performance improvement in today's workplace.

Point System: It is a system where comparing the inter or intra contributions of organizations and assigning a numerical value to each job takes place.

Polarization: It is a condition where a group takes decisions that are extreme than those that would have been taken by group members alone.

Political Risk: It operates at two levels. One is at the project level where the interactions of various groups and administrative agencies in the market will have effects.

The second level is the national and international level. The risk of loss which may occur while investing in a given country arises from the changes in the country's political structure or policies in the form of tax laws, tariffs, expropriation of assets or restrictions in repatriations of profits.

Political Skill: It refers to the ability to effectively understand others at work and to use this knowledge to enhance one's own objectives.

Polycentric Approach: It refers to the approach where the host country nationals are used to staff the subsidiary and the parent company nationals to staff the headquarters.

Polychromic Time Orientation: It refers to comfortable engaging in more than one task at a time that are not troubled by interruptions.

Polygraph Test: Polygraph test is the method of recording physiological activities of human body systems such as respiratory, cardiovascular and sweat glands.

Population: It is the sum total of all elements which represent a group.

Population Trends: Population trends refer to the demographic trends related to the characteristic of people in a certain population.

Porter and Lawler Model: This model explains the complex relationship that exists between motivation, performance and satisfaction.

Position: It refers to the work activities performed by one worker in one establishment.

Position Description/Job Description: It defines general responsibilities of a particular job and also facilitates an evaluation measurement.

Positive Feedback: Positive feedback refers to the information that describes good performance of an employee.

Positive Psychology: It is a movement in psychology initiated in 1998 by *Seligman* and colleagues. *Martin Seligman* is considered to be the father of positive psychology. It emphasizes what is right with people rather than what is wrong with them. According to *Seligman* (2002), the main focus of positive psychology is to understand and facilitate happiness and subjective well being including satisfaction, hope and optimism and flow of happiness.

Positive Reinforcement: It strengthens and increases behaviour by the presentation of a desirable consequence.

Power: *Max Weber* defined power as the probability that one actor within a social relationship will be in a position to carry out his own will despite resistance.

Power Distance: It is the degree to which members of a society expect power to be unequally distributed.

Power Motivation: It can be expressed in the manner which greatly depends upon a person's socio-economic status, sex, level of maturity and the degree to which the individual fears his/her own power motivation. The goal of power motivation is to influence, control, cajole, persuade, lead and charm others and to enhance one's own reputation in the eyes of other people. In other words, it refers to the need to manipulate others or the drive for superiority over others as propagated by *Alfred Adler*.

Predictive Validity: It takes long to establish as criteria lie in the future. This approach puts the decision maker in a precarious position of selecting some people who he/she believes are likely to fail specially those with low test scores.

Prejudice: It refers to unfair negative attitudes we hold about people who belong to social or cultural groups other than our own.

Prescriptive Norms: These are those norms which tell members how to behave.

Pressure: It is the third type of stress which is in the form of expectation and standards which usually one sets for himself/herself or are set by others.

Pressure Tactics: It is using demands, threat, or intimidation to convince someone to comply with a request or to support a proposal.

Prevailing Organizational Culture: It is the pattern of basic assumptions developed by a given group as it learns to cope with its problems.

Primacy Error: It refers to the rating error which occurs when the rater takes performance in the beginning of an assignment into account.

Primary Groups: These are the groups in which interpersonal relationships take place on a face-to-face basis and with great frequency.

Primary Motive: These motives are physiological, biological and unlearned in nature.

Principle of Charity: It occurs when those who have excess should divide it between those who do not have access to it.

Private Employment Agency: It is a form of consultant agency that helps organizations from varied sectors find people for them in return for a commission per candidate.

Private Sector: Private sector includes all sectors outside the government such as for-profit, non-profit, formal and non-formal entities. This broad definition includes service providers, pharmacies, producers and suppliers, shopkeepers and traditional leaders which are not controlled by government.

Proactive Change: A change that is felt desirable by managers. It is a process where the organization actively changes its existing work practices and other areas of work.

Probationer: An individual who is provisionally employed to fill a regular vacancy in a post and has not completed the stipulated probationary period applicable to his/her grade.

Probability: The probability of an event is defined as the relative frequency with which that event would be observed over an infinite number of trials, when each trial is conducted in the same manner.

Problem: It is any conflict between one situation and another situation.

Procedural Justice: Procedural justice refers to the idea of fairness in the processes that resolve disputes and allocate resources.

Procedural Knowledge: It refers to how to do something on routine basis.

Procedural Knowledge and Skill: It refers to the knowledge and skill required to carry out specific tasks.

Process Conflict: It refers to the conflict that arises over responsibilities and how work is completed.

Process Motivation Theory: This theory emphasizes and explains how and why of motivation.

Processual time = Initiation time + Processing time + Time of transaction + Implementation time

Production Teams: These are the teams of the employees who group together to produce tangible products.

Productivity: It refers to a performance measure including effectiveness and efficiency.

Profiles: These are graphical representations of a set of scores for the same individual, expressed in same units of measurement.

Programmed Decisions: These decisions are usually highly structured, i.e. the goals are clear and well-known; the decision making procedure is already established;

and the sources and channels of information are clearly defined, according to *Simon* (1960).

Project/Service Departmentalization: It means categorization of jobs in terms of products and services.

Project Teams: These refer to individuals from different operational areas who get together on a temporary basis to complete a specific project. They are task and time oriented and are dispersed after accomplishment of task.

Projection: It is a mental process in which someone's unwanted motives are shifted on to someone else.

Projective Tests: These tests present undefined, unstructured stimulus situations in the form of pictures, inkblots or incomplete sentences. These are used in clinics and for personnel selections.

Promotion Union: This term refers to those unions in industries, such as cotton spinning and iron and steel, which were developing at the same time as the craft unions but which covered skilled manual workers who were not apprentice-served craftsmen.

Proscriptive Norms: These are the norms that tell members how not to behave.

Pro-social Behaviour: It is being helpful, generous and comforting.

Protean Career: It has been named after *Proteus*, a sea god in Greek mythology who was able to change his shape. The protean career also emphasizes development that is self-directed, continuous, relational and found in challenges at workplace.

Protected Classes: They refer to women, racial minorities who are protected under law against discrimination.

Psyche Group: It is based on a leisure activity criterion.

Psychoanalysis: It was founded in Vienna by *Sigmund Freud*. According to Freud, whatever we do and think results from urges or drives which seek expressions in behaviour and thought.

Psychological Tests: According to *Freeman*, a psychological test is a standardized instrument designed to measure objectively one or more aspects of a total personality by means of a sample of verbal or non-verbal responses or by means of other behaviour.

Psychological Variables: These variables are preferences, needs, value and stereotypes.

Psychological Withdrawal: It is a mental state which withdraws the employee from his/her work.

Psychology: It is the study of human and animal behaviour, including the application of this science to human problems.

Psychophysical System: A psychophysical system is composed of habits, attitudes, emotional status, motives and beliefs which are psychological in nature but they have a physical basis in the individual's neural, glandular or general body states which constitute potential for activity.

Publicness: It refers to the degree of visibility to others.

Public Employment Agency: It is the agency under government control that helps unemployed people find jobs.

Public Sector: The composition of public sector varies country by country. However, in most countries, the public sector includes such services as the police, military, roads, public transport, primary education and healthcare for the poor. In other words, they provide basic government services.

Punishment: It is anything that weakens behaviour and tends to decrease its subsequent frequency.

Purposive Sampling: It means that the researcher has a sample with a particular purpose. The basic assumption behind purposive sampling is that with good judgment and appropriate strategy one can handpick the cases to be included in a sample thus developing samples that are satisfactory in relation to one's needs.

Pygmalion Effect (Self-fulfilling Prophecy): It refers to the behaviour that is adjusted unconsciously to reflect anticipated behaviour in a situation. For example, the employee performance increases when leaders have high expectations about skills and capabilities of employees.

Q

QCC (Quality Control Circle): It refers to a group of individuals who often meet to lay focus upon quality of the task and its related problems.

Qualifications: It refers to the skills, attributes or credentials a person needs to perform each task such as having a BEd degree to teach in a school.

Qualitative Information: It refers to narrative descriptions of work or general statements about working conditions, social context and personnel requirements.

Quality: It is a measure of excellence in product, process and service. In other words, it refers to desired characteristics for product, process and service.

Quantitative Information: It refers to the use of inputs of job information expressed in numerical terms, e.g. ratings of job characteristics, time required or oxygen consumption.

Quick-fix Change: It refers to the attempts at achieving organizational transformation in a short time period, maybe a year or so. These are doomed to fail in long term.

Quid pro quo: In Latin it means 'something for something'. It refers to harassment, asking for sexual favours in return to continued employment or promotion in the organization.

QWL (Quality of Work Life): It aims at creating a conducive and favourable atmosphere required in developing jobs and working environment.

R

Random Sampling: It is a method under which sections of a population are drawn utilizing a procedure by which every member of a population has an equal opportunity to be chosen.

Range: It is the difference between the highest and the lowest score in a distribution.

Rater Bias: It refers to awarding differential ratings to certain groups of people such as women and minorities.

Rating Scale: It is a device that rates social values, official deficiency, group status, etc.

Rationalization: It is about making excuse or giving a reason different from the actual one for what we are doing.

Rational Persuasion: It refers to using logical arguments and factual evidence to persuade someone that a proposal or request is viable and likely to result in the attainment of task objectives.

Rational Strategic Approach: It refers to the situation where the management meticulously plans the strategy before its implementation.

Ratio Scale: It represents all the properties of interval scale and in addition represents an absolute zero point at which there is no heat and no molecular motion.

RCT (Realistic Conflict Theory): It is based on a rational view of humankind. Conflicts between groups are assumed to arise from competition for scarce resources.

RDT (Relative Deprivation Theory): It deals with disadvantaged individuals. It specifies the emotions associated with the feelings of discontent.

Reaction Formation: It is a mental process in which a motive that would arouse unbearable anxiety, if it were recognized, is converted into its opposite.

Reactive Change: It refers to organizational change which is a reaction to some event or situation (privatization, merger, financial crisis, etc). Herein the organization is impelled to change due to forces of change acting upon it.

Reactive Decision Making: It was developed by *Kellie Fowler*. It refers to making good decisions under pressure. People tend to make decisions reactively when confronted with emergency situations. In these circumstances, the best decisions tend to be those that have been thought-through and rehearsed ahead of time.

Reality Check: It refers to the process in which employees determine the accuracy of their self-assessment. They also check as to how those assessments fit with opportunities in the environment.

Realistic Job Preview: It refers to giving a holistic picture about the organization to potential employees.

Realistic Messaging: It refers to messaging both positive and negative features of jobs to potential employees.

Reality Testing: It refers to comparing the stimulus object with other parameters of the same stimulus.

Receiver: The person who receives the message and has the responsibility of decoding it.

Recency Error: Inaccuracy or flaw in performance appraisal caused by the evaluator's reliance on the most recent occurrences of the employee's or the applicant's behaviour. In this the evaluator fails to take into account the entire evaluation period.

Recruiter: An employee of the Human Resource Department who manages the database of resume and carries out research work on job portals, taking initial round of interviews and interacting with the clients.

Rectangular Distribution: A distribution where there are an equal number of cases in all class-intervals.

Redefining Organization: Questioning the core cultural values of the organization as manifested in the mission, structure, technology, psychosocial dynamics, products and services.

Red Tape: It refers to bureaucratic procedures that involve disgusting paper work and routing through endless official channels causing inordinate delays and frustration.

Re-engineering: According to *Hammer* and *Champy*, re-engineering is the fundamental rethinking and radical redesign of business processes to achieve dramatic improvements in critical, contemporary measures of performance, such as cost, speed and service.

Reference Group: This term was given by *Newcomb*. It is used to describe groups in which an individual is a genuine and psychological participant.

References: References contain opinions of people about a candidate's skill, knowledge, and behavioural competence required for the specific job.

Referent Power: This power comes from the desire on the part of the other person to identify with the agent wielding power.

Refreezing: It is a stage wherein leaders employ new approaches by implementing evaluation systems that trace expected behaviour by creating reward systems that reinforce expected behaviours ensuring that recruitment and promotion channels support new demands.

Regiocentric Approach: Carrying out staffing on the basis of the country in which the various subsidiaries are located.

Regression: In the face of threat, one may retreat to earlier patterns of adaptation.

Regression Analysis: It is a mathematical model which states the relation of a dependent variable with an independent variable resulting in regression equation.

Regular Trainees: Regular trainees are hired by the organization for the purpose of imparting training. They sign a training agreement. These trainees do not enjoy the employer-employee relationship.

Reinforcement: It can be defined as anything that increases the strength of response and at the same time tends to induce repetitions of the behaviour that precedes the reinforcement.

Relatedness Need: This need stresses the importance of interpersonal, social relationships.

Relational Commitment: It refers to the commitment based not only on financial incentives but also on social ties.

Relationship Conflict: It is the conflict that arises out of personal differences between people due to differing goals, values, personalities, or the like.

Relative Measures: The performance ratings that assess an employee's inputs by comparing them with the inputs of other employees.

Relevant Variables: The variables which must be considered for control in an experiment.

Reliability Coefficient: It reveals about the effect of measurement error on test scores.

Remuneration Per Employee $= \frac{\text{Basic salary} + \text{Bonus} + \text{Perks}}{\text{Total number of employees}}$

Repatriation: It refers to the process of adjusting to a home country after returning from another country where the individual was living and working.

Repetition: This principle states that a repeated external stimulus is more attention-getting than a single one.

Repression: It is the act of excluding desires and impulses (wishes, fantasies or feelings) from one's consciousness and holding them in the unconscious. Since the popularization of *Sigmund Freud's* work in psychoanalysis, repression is now accepted as a common defence mechanism in everyday life.

Residual Norms: These are the part of implicit norms. These are found out only when they are broken.

Resignation: It occurs when an employee resigns by giving notice in writing to the management.

Resort Hotel: This type of hotel is located in the hills or beaches.

Resource Investigator: It refers to outgoing explorer to liaise outside the team.

Responsibility: This state is concerned with the extent to which employees feel a sense of being personally responsible or accountable for the work being done.

$$\textbf{Retention Rate} = \frac{\text{No. of employees in the company at the end of time period}}{\text{Total number of employees at the start of time period}} \times 100\%$$

Retirement: It occurs when an employee is retired from the services of an organization upon attaining the age of 55 years or as per the rules set by the organization.

Retraining: It occurs in two cases:

- When a system undergoes a change in terms of procedure, equipments being used or the concept of the operation.
- When a new trend has to be incorporated in the existing system of operation.

Revocability: It refers to the ability to change behaviour.

Reward: It is simply something that the person who presents it, deems to be desirable.

Reward Power: This source of power depends on person's ability and resources to reward others.

Risk Analysis: It is like drawing a map of potential hazards and outlining the damage they could cause.

Risk Management: It is taking the risk analysis map and deciding how to avoid the hazards.

Risky Shift: It refers to the process where employees make a risky choice collectively as a group, not while acting alone.

Rites and Rituals: These refer to the public social events that celebrate discrete individual events.

$$\textbf{ROI (Return on Investment)} = \frac{\text{Benefits of training}}{\text{Cost of training}} \times 100$$

Role: It is defined as a position that has expectations evolving from established norms. In other words, it refers to behaviours that define how an individual is supposed to act in a given situation such as workplace or at home.

Role Ambiguity: It arises due to lack of understanding and information available to the role occupant.

Role Boundness: It means an individual feels highly obligated to the expectations of significant role senders, and sacrifices his own interests, preferences, values and comforts for his role.

Role Erosion: It is a subjective feeling which comes when a role occupant feels that some function which he wanted to perform is being performed by some other role occupant.

Role Inadequacy: It refers to two types of feeling:

- Role occupant does not have adequate resources to perform the role effectively.
- He is not fully equipped for effective performance.

Role Isolation: Role isolation arises when there is no frequent interaction between colleagues, resulting in role-role distance.

Role Overload: It occurs when the role occupant feels that there are too many expectations from the significant roles in his role set.

Role Set: It was proposed by *Merton* (1957) as complement of role relationship which persons have by virtue of occupying a particular social status.

Role Stagnation: It includes stress related to career progression.

Rules: These are the strict guidelines related to getting along in the organization.

S

Salary: It is the amount which is received by an employee on weekly, monthly or yearly basis as opposed to an hourly pay. It is a fixed pay according to the employment contract between the employer and the employee.

Sample: It is part of a population which represents the population.

Sampling: It refers to taking any portion of a population as representative of that population in general.

Scalar Chain: It refers to the graded chain of authority from top to bottom through which all communication flows.

Scale Items: In scale items the responses (answers) are put on scale, e.g. agree, somewhat agree, seldom agree and never agree.

Scientific Management: Scientific management focuses on the efficiency and standardization of processes. It is a set of management principles. It is a system devised by industrial engineers for the purpose of serving the common interests of employees, workmen and society at large, through the elimination of avoidable wastes; the general improvement of the processes and methods of production; and scientific distribution of the product. It is the management based upon facts derived from reasoning and systematic observation.

Secondary Motives: These motives are learned, such as need for achievement, power, status, security and affiliation.

Selection Boards: These are more formal and usually larger interviewing panels convened by an official body because there are a number of parties interested in the selection decision.

Selection Interviews: They evaluate the candidates for purposes of hiring, promotion or transfer.

Self Assessment: It refers to the process in which employees determine their interests, values, abilities, aptitude and personality.

Self-concept: It is a person's attempt to understand himself/herself.

Self-efficacy: It is concerned with self perceptions of how well a person can cope with situations as they arise. It is one's perception about oneself that one can successfully execute task and achieve some goals.

Self-esteem: It refers to one's self-perceived competence and self image. It is how individuals perceive themselves in terms of skills, abilities and competencies possessed by them.

Self-orientation: It refers to gaining some self-satisfying ends.

Self-report Method: In this method individuals are asked to express their personal evaluations.

Self-role Distance: It is the conflict between self-concept and the expectations from the role as perceived by the role occupant.

Semi-interquartile Range: It indicates the density of scores at the middle of a distribution.

Sensitivity Training: It is an ODI (Organizational Development Intervention) designed to increase the self-awareness of individuals and their sensitivity towards other people.

Service: It is an activity which is more or less intangible in nature that normally but not necessarily takes place in interaction between the customer and service employees.

Service Team: It refers to the sales team which transacts with customers.

Sexual Harassment: It is referred to unwelcome sexual advances or requests for sexual favours or other verbal/ physical conduct of a sexual nature. Sexual harassment occurs when a victim is approached with unwelcome sexual advances or requests against his/her wishes.

Shaper: A shaper is an aggressive achiever who helps drive a team into action.

SHARP (Stouffer Hotels and Resort's Professional): It is a corporate office-driven programme. It was originally designed for those managers reporting directly to the hotel general manager. The sessions, which typically last five days, include:

- Cost of quality
- Importance of selecting the right individuals as employees
- The cost of turnover and how it affects the bottom line.

Short-term Specialists: These candidates are hired for small periods and they deliver specific labour inputs.

Sick Leave: Sick leave is the leave taken by employees on pretext of being sick or due to injury.

$$\textbf{Sick Leave Rate} = \frac{\text{Number of employees taking sick leave}}{\text{Total number of employees}}$$

Similarity: The law of similarity states about those physical resemblances amongst stimuli which make them perceptually organize as together.

SIPA (Social Information Processing Approach): In this approach, individuals, as adaptive organisms, adopt attitudes, behaviours and beliefs to their social context and to the reality of their own past and present behavioural situations.

SIT (Social Identity Theory): *Commins* and *Lockwood* (1979) stated that a social group is seen to function as a provider of the positive social identity for its members by comparing itself and distinguishing itself from other comparison groups along salient dimensions which have a clear-cut differential.

Situational Contingency Approach: According to *Fiedler*, it is a leadership model in which effectiveness is seen as contingent upon the match of the leader's style with the kind of situation which he/she faces.

Situational Interviews: These interviews focus on what the candidates do in a specific situation. These are based on hypothetical situations, which reflect real life challenging job-related situations. These show how the candidates will handle specific situations.

Six Thinking Hats: It is a powerful technique that helps one look at important decisions from a number of different perspectives and make better decisions by pushing one to move outside the habitual ways of thinking. Many successful people think from a very rational, positive viewpoint, and this is the reason why they are successful. This tool was created by *Edward de Bono* in his book "6 Thinking Hats".

Size (in the context of an organization): It can be referred to insfrastructure (such as floor space, sales volume, clients served, net assets, etc.) or to context (demand). Size often characterises the scale of the work being conducted.

Skill: It refers to the ability to perform a given test with ease and precision. It is any behaviour that has been learned.

Skill-based Pay: It refers to the pay to an employee which is based upon the skills of the employee irrespective of those skills not used by the employee in his/her work domain.

Skill Gap = Required performance – Current performance

Skill Inventories: This is the information that is maintained on the availability and preparedness of non-managerial employees to move into higher level positions or laterally in the organization.

Skill Variety: It refers to the extent to which the job requires the employee to draw from a number of different skills and abilities as well as upon a range of knowledge. It is different from job enlargement. It focuses upon varieties of skills required in the present task rather than performing more tasks requiring the same set of skills.

Social Capital: It represents the resources available to an individual as a result of the individual's personal network of contacts.

Social Facilitation: It refers to the improvement in individual performance when others are present.

Social Impact Theory: *Latane* (1981) proposed that as group size increases, each member feels less and less responsible for the task being performed.

Social Information Processing (SIP) Theory: It is an interpersonal communication theory that suggests that online interpersonal relationship development might require more time to develop than traditional face-to-face relationships.

Social Intelligence: It is the ability to understand and deal with persons.

Social Learning Theory: It was developed by *Albert Bandura*. This theory states that human beings can observe others in a situation and learn from what they see through imitation and modeling and observational learning.

Social Loafing: It refers to a phenomenon wherein people put forth less effort when they work in teams than when they work alone.

Social Motives: These are called social because they are experienced in society. They are complex motive states which are offsprings of human actions.

Social Norms and Expectations: These refer to the knowledge of what others expect from someone.

Socialization: It is a process which teaches and helps one to know what is right and what is wrong.

Society: A society represents the community in which the organization operates.

Sociobiology: *Edward O. Wilson* defines it as the systematic study of the biological basis of all social behaviour.

Socio-group: It is based on a working criterion.

Sociological Variables: Sociological variables are: critical affiliation, age, sex and income.

Source: It refers to the originator of message. It also refers to objects which encode message data and transmit the information via a channel to single or several receivers. There may be several individuals working together as a source.

Span of Control: It refers to the number of subordinates a manager can effectively and efficiently direct.

Special Increment: It occurs when the head of department considers that an employee deserves a special increment. A recommendation for a special increment is made to the HR manager, who in turn submits the proposal to the authorities through Performance Appraisal Form (PAF).

Specialization: It is the extent to which employees have jobs with narrow scopes and limited variety.

Specialist: A specialist is a technical expert who supplies specialized knowledge.

Specific Culture: According to *Trompenaars*, specific culture is the one in which people let others enter their large public space readily but they have a small private space which they guard closely and share only with close friends and associates.

Specific Goals: Specific goals are better than vague or general goals such as "do your best". In other words, the employer giving an employee the exact number of units to produce is preferable than giving vague goals such as "try as hard as you can" or "try to do better than last year".

Split-half Method: It refers to administering the test to a group of individuals and splitting the test into half, in odd-even split.

Staff: The staff gives advice and provides backup and support to the line.

$$\textbf{Staff on Payroll (as percentage of total staff)} = \frac{\text{Number of staff involved in payroll process}}{\text{Total number of employees in the company}} \times 100\%$$

Staffing: It refers to strategically determining, recruiting and hiring the human resources you need for your business.

Stakeholders: Stakeholders are the people who can be employees, customers and owners or shareholders. Their presence affects the organization.

Standard Deviation: By taking the square root of the variance we return to the original units of measurement and thereby obtain a widely used index of variability called the standard deviation.

Standing Plans: Rules and procedures for dealing with issues and tasks that managers face off and on.

Stanine Scores: They have whole number values ranging from 1 to 9. They are used in education. They are a type of normalized standard score.

State Anxiety: According to *Speilberger*, state anxiety refers to transitory emotional states which exist at a given moment in time and at a particular level of anxiety.

Statistic: It is an index that is descriptive of a sample.

Statistics: It is an applied branch of mathematics which classifies, organizes and analyses data.

Stepladder Technique: Making decisions within a group can often be challenging. When things go well, they can go very well. However, when things go wrong, one may end up mired in conflict. The Stepladder Technique is a useful method for encouraging individual participation in group decision making. It encourages all members to contribute on an individual level. This technique is applicable with group having only 4 members. It reduces the risk of social loafing. As the research suggests, decision taking generally loses its effectiveness with a group larger than 9 or 10 people as it loses its productivity and quality of decisions.

Stock: It refers to an incentive that publicly traded firms may choose to offer their employees.

Storming: This stage of development (during group formation) is characterized by conflict and confrontation over roles and duties.

Strain: It refers to the effect of stress on the individual.

Strategic Decision: It emphasizes the means and ends associated with task environment in an organization.

Strategic Gamesman/woman: Such individuals see business life in general and their own career in particular in terms of options and possibilities as if they were playing a game.

Strategic Management: It emphasizes upon planning to produce goods and services and their marketing.

Strategic Partner Role: It is about working with the management of the organization to put the organization's strategies into practice.

Strategic Plan: It is a process of defining the organization's strategy, course of direction and engaging into making decisions for allocating its resources according to its finances and human capital.

Strategy: It refers to the coordinated alternatives and practices that direct employees and organizations.

Stress: According to *Hans Selye* (1956), stress is the condition of the body when it is being influenced by real or imagined pressures.

Stressors: These are environmental conditions that cause individuals to experience stress.

Strike: It is the refusal of union members to work. A strike is recognized as a basic union right.

Structured Interviews: In structured interviews, the interview schedule is pre-planned and questions are asked in an order according to the pre-planned format.

Structured Problem: A structured problem is the one which is stated in a context and is well-defined and clear.

Structural Redesign: It is an ODI (Organizational Development Intervention) that involves re-aligning the structure of the organization to improve performance. This includes examining the best fit between structure technology and environment.

Subcultures: Subcultures in the organizational context refer to the groups that share such values that differ from the main values of the organization.

Sublimation: It refers to a mental process which redirects emotional impulses to socially valued activities and goals.

Subliminal Perception: A subliminal message is a signal or message embedded in another object, designed to pass below the normal limits of perception. Subliminal messages are indiscernible by the conscious mind, but affect the subconscious or deeper mind. Subliminal techniques have occasionally been used in advertising.

Substance Abuse: It is the overindulgence in a chemical or dependence on a drug leading to effects that are detrimental to an individual's physical and mental health as well as the welfare of others.

Substance Abusing Employees: Those employees who abuse alcohol and drug and thus require increased health insurance leading to lost productivity and injuries.

Suburban Hotel: This type of hotel is located in suburbs having quieter surroundings. Rates are quoted as moderate to low.

Succession Planning: It is a career development activity that focuses on preparing people to fill executive positions.

Suggestion: It is uncritical acceptance of a statement.

Supervisory training: It is the training in management.

Supportive Leadership: The leader shows concern and support for subordinates.

Survey Feedback: It is an ODI (Organizational Development Intervention) which begins with the collection of data via questionnaires from organization members or a representative sample of them. Then the data is presented to the members. They engage together to interpret the data and develop action plans in response.

Survey Technique: It is one of the techniques to study large and small samples to discover the relative incidence, distribution and inter-relation of sociological and psychological variables.

Swift Trust: It occurs when early communication is task-focused, positive and reciprocated, i.e. questions and inputs do not go unanswered.

SWOT Model (strengths, weaknesses, opportunities and threats): It is a decision making tool where strengths and weaknesses are identified, opportunities are perceived and threats are taken note of. It can be presented in a two by two matrix. The four quadrants provide an effective framework for reviewing strategy, position and direction of the organization's status, etc. This method can be used in conjunction with other decision making techniques.

Strengths	Weaknesses
Opportunities	Threats

Syndicate Approach: A syndicate approach should be encouraged because the coordinator need not be present during the deliberations of the syndicate. This enables quiet students to open up. Different members in the syndicate bring different specializations into the discussion and each participant would benefit by listening to the arguments of other syndicate members. Participants may be able to ask questions in a smaller group and appreciate the different approaches of the fellow participants.

Synergy: It refers to total amount of energy available for expenditure.

Syntality: It refers to total performance of a group.

Systematic Observation: It is an alternative of experimental method, where independent variables are not manipulated by the researcher. In fact, they capitalize on variables that occur.

Systems Analysis: It is a deductive procedure. It is a step-by-step logical subdivision of the total task of the organization. It begins with a specification of the overall task.

T

Three-sixty-degree Feedback: It is a method of performance appraisal where feedback is obtained from colleagues, peers, immediate boss and even customers.

TA (Transactional Analysis): It was developed by *Eric Berne* (1970), who called it a theory and a method of social psychiatry. As a theory of personality, TA gives us a picture of how people are structured psychologically using the three-part ego state model.

Tabulation: Counting, taking out proportion or calculating percentages to analyze the information is called tabulation. In tabulation results show the pattern.

Tacit Knowledge: The knowledge that cannot be recorded or documented and whose tangibility is only ephemerally perceptible. When the knowledge is tacit, it becomes difficult for a firm to truly know what it is, in the process of acquiring it. Tacit knowledge is also difficult to preserve or use to construct a competitive advantage.

Tactical Plan: It outlines the implementation phase of the planning process, usually for one to two years.

Talent War: It refers to negative competition in which poaching exists.

Tall Organization: It is a structure where there is a series of narrow spans of control.

Targeted Skill Scope: It refers to a recruiting strategy that seeks to attract only those who have specific attributes.

Task: A task is a work activity that has a reasonably definitive purpose and that can usually be clearly identified as a segment of the work of a particular job. In other words, it refers to actions to accomplish an objective. It refers to what an individual you hire would actually do, for example, driving your car, keeping your phone working, etc.

Task Analysis: It is the analysis of how a task is accomplished by considering both physical and cognitive abilities. According to *Jonassen*, *Tessmer* and *Hannum,* task analysis for instructional design is a process of analyzing and articulating the kind of learning that you expect the learners to know to perform their tasks.

Task Analysis Inventory: It is a method of job analysis in which the job incumbents rate the frequency and importance of the tasks associated with a specific set of work duties.

Task Conflict: It is a conflict that involves work content and goals. Task conflicts involve disagreements among team members on performance related activities.

Task Environment : It consists of the external environment which includes allies, customers, competitors and suppliers.

Task Identity: It refers to whether the job has an identifiable beginning and end.

Task Inventories/Job Inventories: These consist of a list of tasks pertinent to any occupational area such as health or automobile. In completing an inventory for any given position within an occupational area, each task is either checked or rated as it applies to the position. The rating is in accordance with any of the rating factors such as:

- The frequency with which the task is performed.
- The time spent on the task.
- Its judged importance or significance.

Task Orientation: It refers to the attitude of getting the job done.

Task Performance: It refers to the employee inputs that directly contribute to outputs in the form of producing goods or services.

Task Significance: It involves the importance of the task. It involves both internal significance as to how important the task is to the organization and the external significance as to how proud the employees are to tell their relatives and friends about what, how and where they work.

Task Synergy: It is the energy expended to execute the group's task, and for attainment of the group goals and objectives.

Team: It is an integrated social entity whose members share common objective, work towards common goal and manage their interpersonal relationship across organizational hierarchies.

Team Worker: A team worker is a socially skilled harmonizer to defuse conflict.

Technical Skills: These skills refer to one's ability to apply specialized knowledge or expertise.

Technical Training: It refers to training in technical aspects of job.

Technology: It refers to how an organization transfers its inputs into outputs.

Telecommunication: It refers to the use of telephone and television technologies and a wireless system of portable phones as well as a wired system built around fiber-optic links.

Telecommuting: It refers to a work situation in which employees on a regular, predetermined basis spend all or a portion of their work week by operating from home or another non-organization site.

Telephone Surveys: These surveys are conducted on phone. They are very convenient and economical but not very effective as some people may not readily give information.

Telework: It refers to performing work via the Internet and phone.

Temporary: It refers to an individual who has been temporarily engaged for work which is likely to be determined within a limited period.

Temporary and Part-time Working: It allows the individuals to choose the amount of time that they want to devote to a particular employer.

Termination: When permanent employees are asked to resign by the management, it is deemed that the employee's services have been terminated. When the resignation of an employee is accepted by the management without notice, it is followed by the termination process.

Test-retest Method: It directly assesses the degree to which test scores are consistent from one test administration to the next.

T-group (Laboratory training): It involves training that leads to attitudinal change, which contributes to understanding of self and change in the organization. It helps us know about team building. In T-groups, participants learn about themselves through their interaction with each other. A T-group meeting does not have an explicit agenda or structure. Under the guidance of a facilitator, the participants are encouraged to share with the group their emotional reactions such as anger, fear, warmth or envy, which arise in response to their fellow participants' actions and statements. The emphasis is on sharing emotions, as opposed to judgments or conclusions.

The Kepner-Tregoe Matrix: It provides an unbiased, efficient, systematic, step-by-step framework for gathering, organizing and evaluating decision making information. It is also called root cause analysis. This approach was developed by *Charles H. Kepner* and *Benjamin B. Tregoe* in the 1960s. There are four steps which form a process of decision making:

Situation appraisal (1st step)

↓

Problem appraisal (2nd step)

↓

Decision appraisal (3rd step)

↓

Potent problem appraisal (4th step)

The Ladder of Inference: It was initially developed by *Chris Argyris.* In today's fast-moving world, a person is always under pressure to act now, rather than spend time reasoning things through and thinking about the true facts. Not only can this lead us to a wrong conclusion, but it can also cause conflict with other people, who may have drawn quite different conclusions on the same matter. So when a person accepts or challenges other people's conclusions, he/she needs to be confident that their reasoning is firmly based on the true facts. The ladder of inference helps achieve this.

Action taken

Beliefs formed

Conclusions drawn

Assumptions formed

Meanings added

Data selected

Observable Data Experience

The Vroom-Yetton-Jago Decision Model: This model was originally described by *Victor Vroom* and *Philip Yetton* in their book titled "Leadership and Decision Making". Later, in 1988, *Vroom* and *Arthur Jago* replaced the decision tree system of the original model with an expert system based on mathematics. Hence the model is called Vroom-Yetton-Jago model. This decision making model enables the leader to appraise the situation so that he/she can decide which style or extent of involvement is required. This model is spread along a continuum ranging from autocratic to consultative to group-based participation.

Continuum

Autocratic | Consultative | Group-based participation

Theory: It is a set of systematically inter-related concepts or hypotheses that purports to explain and predict a phenomenon.

Theory X: It refers to the assumption that employees dislike work and responsibility. They are lazy and must be coerced to perform.

Theory Y: It refers to the assumption that employees like work. They are innovative, seek to hold responsibility and need a supportive environment for the sake of optimal performance.

Theory Z: This theory is based upon Japanese and American practices. Theory Z focuses on increasing the employee loyalty to the company by providing a job for life with a strong focus on the well-being of the employee, both on and off the job. Theory Z management tends to promote stable employment.

Thick Culture: An organizational culture is said to be thick if it is widespread and accepted throughout the organization, and organizational members subscribe to a shared set of beliefs, norms and values.

Thin Culture: It is one that is not widely held and does not enjoy acceptance throughout the organization. The organization lacks a core of commonly held beliefs, norms and values.

Thinking: It is a form of information processing that goes on during the period between a stimulus event and the response to it.

Third Country Nationals: They refer to neither citizens of the home country nor of the host country.

Thomas Profiling Hiring Technique: It is a psychological test which is used for selecting employees and also classifies the domain on which employee can be trained once selected.

Threat: It refers to anticipated harm from a potential source.

Threshold Traits Analysis: It is a job analysis method that provides normative data on the worker attributes required for successful job performance.

$$\textbf{Time Taken to Fill a Job Vacancy} = \frac{\text{Total number of days from initiation to recruiting}}{\text{Number of recruits}}$$

Tinkering: It refers to the process of making occasional, unrelated, and relatively minor organizational changes in the hope of improved performance.

TNA (Training Needs Analysis): It refers to an examination of the organization's present and expected operations and the manpower necessary to carry them out, in order to identify the number and categories of staff needing to be trained or retrained. It may also refer to the training needs of an individual to enable him/her to reach the required standard of performance in his/her current state or future job.

TQM (Total Quality Management): It is an organizational strategy with accompanying techniques that delivers quality products and services to customers.

Trade Unions: These are voluntary organizations of workers formed to promote and protect their interests through collective action.

$$\textbf{Trained Employee Percentage in Specific Grade} = \frac{\text{Number of employees receiving training in specific grade}}{\text{Total number of employees who received training}}$$

Trainee: A trainee is an individual engaged for being imparted in-house training in specific trades under a training agreement. Trainees do not enjoy employer-employee relationship.

Training: It is a planned effort to impart job-related knowledge, skills and attitude to employees. It is a process of attitudinal change that integrates with life, work and development of self. It focuses on general requirements across job/role profile in an organization. It is vocationally oriented and occurs in work organizations or educational institutions.

$$\textbf{Training Hours Per Employee} = \frac{\text{Total number of training hours for all employees}}{\text{Total number of employees}}$$

Training Media: It refers to the means by which contents and methods of training are delivered to the trainees.

Trait Anxiety: It refers to relatively stable individual differences in anxiety-proneness, i.e. differences between people in the tendency to perceive a stressful situation as dangerous or threatening, according to *Speilberger*.

Trait Theory of Leadership: This theory states that leaders are born, not made. It is the traits like sociability, intelligence, etc. that decide who is a leader.

Transformational Change: It involves challenging all the assumptions underlying existing organizational arrangements, which result in a profound change.

Transactional Commitment: It refers to the commitment based on financial incentives rather than social ties.

Transnational Corporation: It refers to a firm that attempts to balance local responsibilities and global scale via a network of specialized operating units.

Transformational Leadership: Such leaders possess the capability to motivate employees to look beyond their self-interest for the benefit of individual work groups and the organization as a whole by inspiring, energizing, intellectually stimulating and consistently demonstrating espoused organizational values in their actions and behaviour.

Transactional Leadership: It refers to a leadership style that is based on the exchange relationship between the subordinates and the leader.

Transfer to Training: It occurs when the employees apply their training to their jobs.

Truth-wins Scheme: As more information is provided and opinions are discussed, the group comes to recognize that one approach is objectively correct.

t-score: It is not normally distributed because in the denominator there is a variable. It is more leptokurtic (distribution with positive kurtosis) than the normal distribution.

$$t = \frac{\text{(Normally distributed)} - \text{(Constant)}}{\text{(Variable)}}$$

Turnaround Strategy: It refers to the competitive business strategy which focuses upon radical change which equips the organization to achieve the state of profitability.

Turnover: It refers to voluntary and involuntary permanent withdrawal from the organization.

Turnover Cost Incurred by Recruitment Department=

$$\left(\frac{\text{Withdrawn offers}}{\text{Total no. of offers made}}\right) \times (\text{Recruiting costs})$$

$$\left[\left(\frac{\text{No. of employees leaving within 3 months}}{\text{Total no. of offers made}}\right) \times \begin{matrix}(\text{Recruiting costs} + \\ \text{Training costs} + \\ \text{Salary and benefits})\end{matrix}\right]$$

$$+ \text{Replacement} - \text{Time costs}$$

Two-thirds Majority Scheme: This scheme is frequently adopted by juries, who tend to convict the defendants when two-thirds of the jury initially favours conviction.

Type 'A' Personality: The people with type 'A' personality are competitive, restless, high achieving, active, aggressive and identified as "go-getter".

Type 'B' Personality: People with this type of personality are less motivated, relaxed and relatively free of pressures.

U

Unemployment: It is a condition of being out of work. In other words it is being jobless, unable to pay bills, rent or meet financial obligations.

Unemployment Compensation: It was started in 1935 by the *Social Security Act* to provide security to employees who became unemployed for no fault of their own.

Uniform Transactional Compensation: It refers to the reward package that uses money to build commitment. It works towards minimizing the differences in the pay levels of employees.

Union Shop: It refers to the situation where the employees are required to join the union as soon as they complete the joining formalities. A union shop does not require employees to be union members as a condition of employment, but does require that they join the union or pay the equivalent of union dues within a set period of time following their hire.

Union Steward: Such a person is an advocate or representative of the labour union.

Unity of Command: Unity of command helps preserve the concept of an unbroken line of authority. It means that a person should have one and only one supervisor to whom she/he is directly responsible.

Universalism: *Trompenaars* defined it as the belief that ideas and practices can be applied everywhere without modification.

Universalistic Approach: It is a perspective that identifies the ways to manage people that prove to be effective across all organizations.

Unstructured Interviews: These are those interviews in which the interview schedule is not pre-planned. The interviewer can ask any question in any order.

Upward Appeal: Upward appeal is persuading a person that the request is approved by higher management or appealing to higher management for assistance in gaining his/her compliance with the request.

Upward Communication: It refers to the communication that flows from subordinates to the top management.

V

Validity: It is one of the most essential characteristics of a standardized test. A test is valid in two conditions:

- When it measures what it is supposed to measure. It is known as validity for measurement.
- How far the test scores can be used to predict and make accurate decisions? It is known as validity of decisions.

Values: Values refer to abstract ideals related to proper life goals and methods for reaching those goals.

Valuing Diversity: It refers to awareness, recognition, understanding and appreciation of human differences. It takes place through training and development of employees to improve interpersonal relationships among diverse groups.

Variable: Any particular observation is called a value of the variable.

Variable Pay Technique: It is an intermittent type of reinforcement schedule and attempts to reward according to individual or group differences. Variable pay is also referred to as "Pay at risk".

Variance: It can be defined as the mean of squares of the deviation scores. It is denoted as sigma square.

Vertical Alignment: It refers to the state in which an organization's human resource strategy supports its competitive business strategy.

Vested: It refers to the eligibility upon which the individual is entitled to receive retirement benefits, but it can only be availed after working for a certain period of time.

Vestibule Training: Vestibule training is a simulated on-the-job training.

Virtual Organization: It is an organization whose members are geographically apart yet connected through computer networks. It is a company that outsources most of its functions and highly skilled workers work in a collaborative climate.

Virtual Teams: These are the teams that rely heavily on electronically mediated communication rather than face-to-face meetings as the means to coordinate work.

Vision: It is a statement of what the organization aspires in the forthcoming period.

Vocational Tests: These tests are used to assess what profession will suit the person who takes the test taking into account his/her interest, personality, aptitude and abilities.

Voluntary Association: A voluntary association is formed as per an agreement by a group of individuals to accomplish a purpose.

$$\textbf{Voluntary Rate} = \frac{\text{Number of employees leaving voluntarily}}{\text{Total number of employees within a specific period}}$$

Voluntary Turnover: It is a situation where the employee chooses to leave the organization at his/her own free will.

Vroom's Expectancy Theory of Motivation: *Vroom* proposed his expectancy theory as an alternative to content models. It is built around the concepts of valence, instrumentality and expectancy.

- **Valence** means the strength of an individual's preference for a particular outcome.
- **Expectancy** relates efforts to first-level outcomes.
- **Instrumentality** relates first-level outcomes and second-level outcomes.

W

Wage: Wages include salary, bonuses, incentives and commission paid by an employer to an employee for his/her services. It is a remuneration which the employee receives in exchange for the specified quantity of his/her labour.

Web-based Training: It is a non-profit group for employees, people and employers interested in developing and delivering training through the Internet.

Whistle Blowing: It refers to the disclosure of an employee's immoral, unethical and illegitimate code of conduct. The whistleblower can be internal and external. The internal whistleblower is an employee who reports misconduct by another employee to his/her senior. The external whistleblower reports matter to the outside agency such as media, lawyer or watchdog agencies.

Work Activities: It is a general term that refers to virtually any of the physical actions or mental processes by which workers achieve intended job objectives.

Workforce: It includes all those employed in a specific organization and all those available for work.

Work-life Balance (WLB) : This term was coined by *David Clutterbuck* in 1986. He defines it as:

- Being aware of different demands on time and energy.
- Having the ability to make choices in the allocation of time and energy.
- Knowing what values to apply to choices.
- Making choices.

Workload: It is a hypothetical relationship between a working group and task requirements.

Work Psychology: It is referred to as human resource management. It is also referred to as industrial psychology. Work psychology is primarily concerned with issues that are of molecular nature. It focuses on issues such as human resource planning; job analysis; descriptions and specifications; recruitment and selection; training and development; compensation and benefits; performance appraisal and career development plan and implementation.

Work Role Centrality: It refers to the extent to which an individual's life situations move around his/her job.

Work Specialization: It refers to the degree to which tasks in the organization are subdivided into separate jobs.

Work Teams: They provide greater flexibility, reduce operating costs, enhance technological change, strengthen the ability to attract and retain cream of talent, and facilitate innovation by bringing together experts with different knowledge perspectives.

Work-to-family Conflict: It refers to the fact that meeting work obligations causes some problems which negatively influence an individual's behaviour at home.

XYZ

Yuppies: These are urbanites who are successful professionals focused upon making money and spending on electronic appliances and toys.

ZBB (Zero Base Budgeting): It aims to achieve optimum allocation of resources which incremental and other budgeting systems cannot achieve. ZBB combines planning and budgeting into a single process. It is a method of budgeting which starts from zero base in which all expenses are justified for the new period.

Zeigarnik Effect: It was given in 1927 by *Zeigarnik*. It refers to the phenomenon of better memory for unfinished or interrupted tasks.

Z-score: It is a standard score. The researcher makes use of it to represent the area of normal curve. It states the position of a score in relation to the mean of the distribution, using standard deviation (SD) as units of measurement, i.e. by how many SD points the corresponding raw score lies above or below the mean of the distribution. It is normally distributed because in the denominator there is a constant.

$$\mathbf{Z} = \frac{\text{(Normally Distributed Variable)} - \text{(Constant)}}{\text{(Constant)}}$$

Abbreviations

A : Autonomy

AC : Affective Commitment

AHP : Analytic Hierarchy Process

BARS : Behaviourally Anchored Rating Scale

BCG Matrix : The Boston Consulting Group

BEST : Building Effective Sales Technique

BPO : Business Process Outsourcing

BOS : Behaviour Observation Scale

CAI : Computer Assisted Instruction

CDE : Competency Development Expense

DOT : Dictionary of Occupational Titles

DV : Dependent Variable

EAP : Employee Assistance Programme

EEO : Equal Employment Opportunities

EII : Employee Involvement Index

EIS : Executive Information System

EPPA : Employees Polygraph Protection Act

ESOP : Employee Stock Ownership Plan

EQ/EI : Emotional Quotient/ Emotional

	Intelligence
F	: Feedback
FJA	: Functional Job Analysis
FP	: Focal Person
FR	: Forced Ranking
GAS	: General Adaptive Syndrome
GSI	: Guest Satisfaction Index
HC	: Human Capital
HRD	: Human Resource Development
HRIS	: Human Resource Information System
IHRM	: International Human Resource Management
JCM	: Job Characteristic Model
KPI	: Key Performance Indicator
KRA	: Key Result Area
LPC	: Least Preferred Co-worker
MBO	: Management By Objectives
MIS	: Management Information System
MNC	: Multinational Corporation
MPS	: Motivating Potential Score
MT	: Management Trainee
MTOP	: Management Training On Property
N-Ach	: Need for Achievement
NGO	: Non-governmental Organization
NGT	: Nominal Group Technique
OB	: Organizational Behaviour
OB Mod.	: Organizational Behaviour Modification
OD	: Organizational Development
ODI	: Organizational Development Intervention

OJE	: Orthodox Job Enrichment
PA	: Performance Appraisal
PAQ	: Position Analysis Questionnaire
PDCA	: Plan, Do, Check, and Act
PEM	: Punctuated Equilibrium Model
PEST	: Political, Economic, Social and Technology Analysis
PMI	: Plus Minus Interesting
POB	: Positive Organizational Behaviour
QC	: Quality Control Circles
QWL	: Quality of Work Life
RCT	: Realistic Conflict Theory
RDT	: Relative Deprivation Theory
ROI	: Return on Investment
SD	: Standard Deviation
SHARP	: Stouffer Hotels and Resort's Professional
SIPA	: Social Information Processing Approach
SIT	: Social Identity Theory
SPC	: Statistical Process Control
SV	: Skill Variety
SWOT	: Strengths, Weaknesses, Opportunities and Threats
TA	: Transactional Analysis
TNA	: Training Needs Analysis
TQM	: Total Quality Management
WLB	: Work Life Balance
ZBB	: Zero Based Budgeting

❑

Section III

HR Documents

Introduction to HR Documents

The following table states the name of various HR documents used in an organization along with their intended use.

S No	Name of the HR Document	Purpose/Use
1.	Resume	It is that document which showcases the credentials of a person. It makes him/her eligible for the job or not. It is a personalized document and that which keeps on growing. It is the first and most important document for every department, especially HR. If a person is not selected for the present position and found suitable then his/her resume goes into the file of future reference. There are job sites which bank upon large storage of resumes. To post a resume or to track resumes, membership of a related job site is essential. Today a job website is a business worth crores. To maintain the record of resumes on the Internet or manually in cardboard files, a separate cell or department of recruitment is required. Recruitment is that cell of the Human Resources Department from where the process of one's employment starts & finishes.

Contd. on next page

contd from previous page

S No	Name of the HR Document	Purpose/Use
2.	Interview Record Form	To collect the information about the candidate.
3.	Interview Work Sheet	To document the process of interview.
4.	Application Blank	To maintain personal records of the personnel working in the organization.
5.	Offer Letter	To give intimation of joining to the individual.
6.	Welcome Letter	To show the beginning and mark the orientation of new recruits.
7.	Appointment Letter	To make the selected person to accept the conditions to join the company.
8.	Confirmation Letter	To document that the employee's service with the organization is confirmed immediately after the appointment or after a period of probation.
9.	Attendance Sheet	To document and use information regarding an employee's attendance at work and absence from work for payroll processing task.
10.	Job Description	To frame KRAs (Key Result Areas) of an employee.
11.	Personnel Requisition Form	To act as a facilitator in the process of HRP (Human Resource Planning/ Manpower Planning).
12.	Business Ethics & Conduct	Part of the compliance policy of the organization Disclosure Statement
13.	Training Schedule	It is a calendar which showcases various trainings to take place/have taken place in the organization by the trainers on scheduled dates.
14.	Training Feedback Form	To make the training more effective.

Contd. on next page

Contd. from previous page

S No	Name of the HR Document	Purpose/Use
15.	MBO (Management by Objective) Form	To state the KRAs (Key Result Areas) of an employee to reach the desired performance.
16.	Annual Appraisal Form	To reward the employee through compensation and benefits and promote to a higher position or demote the employee based on his/her performance.
17.	Increment Letter	To document the credit of the employee.
18.	Letter of Appreciation	To document the credit of the employee.
19.	Leave Format	To avail leaves during the said period out of the specified number of leaves so that excess leaves cannot be taken.
20.	Illness/Injury Form	To document the absenteeism.
21.	Experience Certificate	To show credentials of an individual.
22.	Exit Interview Form	To understand what went wrong with the employee with regard to career development plan (CDP), interpersonal relations, organizational culture, climate and compensation & benefits.
23.	Final Relieving Letter	To show that the employee's account closed in the organization.

Form 1: Resume/Curriculum Vitae

Name:

Sex : D.O.B :

Contact Details : (Address)

Contact nos.

Subject :

Objective :

Professional Experience :

Research Experience :

Professional Qualification :

(Also state curriculum of your specialization)

Educational Qualifications & Achievements :

- Master's in

  From :

  Percentage :

- Bachelor's in

  From :

  Percentage :

- Schooling from :

  State percentage of X and XII :

Other Curriculum Achievements:

Interest Areas :

Strengths :

Weaknesses :

Signature :

Date :

Form 2: Interview Record Form
Annexure 1

Company Name:

Date:

Reference:

Initial Score Card No.

Name:

Age: Sex:

Contact nos.:

Education:

Professional training:

Work History:

Communication:

Any other information:

Signature of the Appraiser:

Comments:

Form 3: Interview Work Sheet
Annexure 2

Present Salary: Expected Salary:

Position Applied for:

Name:

Age: Sex: Marital status:

Type Assessment:

Results of psychometric tests:

Rating Scale:

Poor (P) Average (A) Good (G) Very Good (VG)

a. Driven for results
b. Functional excellence
c. Goal orientation
d. Customer focus
e. People development skills
f. Withstanding pressure
g. Shared vision and mission
h. Team spirit
i. Grooming

Remarks by interviewer

1. Name:
   Position:
   Signature: Date:
2. Name:
   Position:
   Signature: Date:
3. Name:
   Position:
   Signature: Date:
   Decision:
   Rejected/Selected Future Reference

Signature by all appraisers

Form 4: Application Blank

Name :

Age: Sex: Marital Status:

Present Address:

Permanent Address:

Telephone No.:

Position Applied for:

Where did you learn of this vacancy?

Family members' description and their occupation:

What academic/professional qualifications do you hold?
(Use initials to indicate this, e.g. BSc, MBA, MCA, 10+2, etc.)

Secondary Education:

Dates	Name of School/Board	Give details of major subjects studied	Examinations taken & results

Contd. on next page

Contd. from previous page

Education beyond Secondary Level:

Dates	Name of Institution/ University	Give details of major subjects studied	Examinations taken & results

Training:

(Give details of any specialized training received and /or courses attended)

Other Skills:

(Other qualifications & skills including languages, current driving licence, keyboard skill, etc.)

Employee History

(Give details here of all positions held since completing your full time education. Start with your present or most recent position and work back.)

Dates	Name of Employer, address, nature of business	Starting & leaving positions Salary & Benefits	Reason for leaving or wanting to leave

Contd. on next page

Contd. from previous page

Interests

Please describe your leisure interests

Additional Information & Comments:

Do you have any permanent or persistent health problems? Please give details.

Have you ever worked for this company?

Please state salary expected.

When would you be able to start work, if offered a position?

Do you have a car to travel to work? What is the nature of conveyance, specify?

Any commitments outside work, which could influence your decision in taking a job?

Personal time scales for finding a suitable job

Very urgent	High active
Low active	Casual

Why do you want to work for this company?

How & why is it important for you to join this company?

Why do you want to leave your present job?

For one to perform a job successfully what would you think are the essential components?

Work Preferences

(Please specify in terms of an ideal job, top 5 criteria defining attitude to team work, use of initiative, level of responsibility, personal contact, i.e. work pace sought, flexibility, etc)

Contd. on next page

Contd. from previous page

Work Habits

(Specify your work habits in terms of management style, decision making, cooperation, and problem solving.)

Please list your strengths and weaknesses.

Add any comments you wish to make to support your application

Please give the names & addresses of two persons who are in a position to comment on your professional/ work ability

Name	Name
Address	Address
Tel. No.:	Tel. No.:
Position	Position
Known since	Known since
Relation	Relation

I confirm that the information given on this application form is correct.

Signature of Applicant Date

Form 5: Offer Letter

VVV Technologies
P.O. Box 000
X City
Y State
000 000

Date

QQQ

123 Cross City

Dear QQQ

Subject: Job Offer

VVV Technologies is pleased to offer you a job as a Sr. Project Manager. We trust that your knowledge, skills and experience will be among our most valuable assets.

Should you accept this job offer, as per organization's policy you'll be eligible to receive the following compensation and benefits at the start of your hire date.

Compensation

- Salary – Annual gross starting salary of Rs. 2.5 lacs by your choice of cheque or direct deposit.
- Bonus – Up to 3% of your annual gross salary will be paid annually by your choice of cheque or direct deposit.
- Benefits – VVV Technologies provide:
    - Children education assistance
    - Health, life and disability insurance
    - Profit sharing
    - Vacation & personal days.

Accept It

1. Put sign and date on this offer letter as indicated.

Contd. on next page

Contd. from previous page

2. Do sign and date the enclosed Confidentiality Agreement as indicated.
3. Complete all the formalities that confirms your acceptance of offer letter by VVV Technologies.

Decline It

1. Put sign and date on this offer letter as indicated
2. Do inform the management about your decision.

We at VVV Technologies hope that you'll accept this offer of employment with us and look forward to meet you at the orientation meet.

Sincerely,

AAA

HR Director

Enclosures ....

Accept job offer

Signature Date

Decline job offer

Signature Date

Form 6: Welcome Letter

Dear ,

Welcome to XYX Ltd.

I am pleased that you have chosen to accept our offer of employment and I take pleasure in welcoming you to the organization.

Our goal is to be India's biggest & best organization with a crores turnover. We look forward to your association and contribution in achieving our goals.

Our organizational induction is targeted towards providing you with clarity on our history, organizational structure, organizational culture and the organization's policies and procedures. Your assigned mentor will help you through your initial phase at XYX Ltd.

You join an exceptional group of individuals who have performed beyond boundaries, who believe in leadership through differentiation.

I wish you the best in your career with XYX.

Regards,

Authorized by:

Name

Designation

Organization's Name

Date:

Form 7: Appointment Letter

Date

Name

Dear Mr/Ms

With reference to your application and interview followup with us, we are pleased to appoint you as (designation) in our company on the following terms and conditions.

- Joining Date:
- Salary: Your annual total cost to the company would be .... and details of benefits and salary are given in the Annexure attached below.
- Location transfer: You are appointed, as .... and posted at .... but if required you shall be liable to be posted or transferred anywhere to serve any of the organization's assignments and responsibilities to be fulfilled by you. It is based at the sole discretion of the management.
- Probation/confirmation: Your probation period will be of six months. Your performance will confirm your status after six months of probation period. During this period your services can be terminated with seven days of notice whatsoever the reason would be.
- Absence for a continuous period of (no. of days) without intimation and approval by the immediate supervisor may result in losing the job as per the organization's policy.

Contd. on next page

Contd. from previous page

- During the period of employment you are required to devote full time to the work. You cannot take up any other employment or project for any cash or kind without the written permission of the management of the organization.

Terms and conditions are stated below:

1. You are required to comply with all rules and regulations as per the organization's policy and procedure.
2. You will be required to keep project documents, software packages, licence, company's policies, formats, trade mark, cost and estimation records and HR documents as confidential. Any document or important information given to you during the continuance of your service should be kept secret.
3. You cannot publish any article, give statements, and deliver any lecture or broadcast relating to the organization's products and services unless you have been granted permission to do so.
4. You cannot accept any present, commission or any article in cash or kind from any person, agency or company who deal with the organization. If offered by someone then you are required to report the matter to the management of the organization. Further, if your behaviour found to be dishonest, disobedient, and disorderly; your performance is evaluated as poor; and you are found to be absenting from job without prior information — all this may lead to your termination from the service and any damage to the property or assets of the organization caused by you will be recovered from you.
5. This appointment letter is issued on the basis of the information and particulars presented by you

Contd. on next page

Contd. from previous page

in bio-data, during interview and in the application blank of the organization. If this information is found to be false then the management will take action against non-transparency, and it will result in termination of your services with the organization.

Please sign and return to the undersigned the duplicate copy of this appointment letter notifying your acceptance of the said rules and employment with us.

We welcome you to the organization .... and look forward a beneficial collaboration.

With best wishes

Authorized by:

Name

Designation

Organization name

Date

Form 8: Confirmation Letter

Date

Name

Emp. No.

Designation

Department

Dear Mr/Ms

We are pleased to inform you that your performance has been found satisfactory and hence we are happy to inform you that your service has been confirmed with effect from .... and your revised emoluments are ....

However, other terms and conditions remain the same.

We look ahead to your satisfactory performance as per continuation of employment with us.

Kindly intimate your acceptance by putting signature on this letter and in duplicate also and return it to the HR Department of the organization.

Yours sincerely,

Authorized by:

Name

Designation

Signature of the employee

Form 9: Job Description Format

Basic information

a. Job incumbent's name
b. Position title
c. Grade
d. Reporting officer
e. Position vacant
(Name of the branch)

Purpose of the position

Task reporting structure

Key Result Areas (KRAs)

Professional experience

Skills

Form 10: Attendance Format

This format can be put on an Excel sheet with the following headers, like P for present, A for absence, L for leave, W for weekly off, H for holidays and O for overtime. And in the end appropriate formulae can be used for payroll processing.

Employee code

Employee Name

Designation

Department

Date of Joining

March 2009

Sun	Mon	Tue	Wed	Thu	Fri	Sat
1	2	3	4	5	6	7
H	**P**	**P**	**P**	**P**	**P**	**H**
8	9	10	11	12	13	14
H	**A**	**A**	**P**	**P**	**P**	**H**
15	16	17	18	19	20	21
H	**P**	**P**	**L**	**P**	**P**	**O**
22	23	24	25	26	27	28
W						**W**
29	30	31				
H	**P**	**P**				

Form 11: Personnel Requisition Form

To:

From:

Department:

Position required:

No. of vacancies:

(In the same department)

No. of positions:

Job description:

Skills required:

Candidate's specifications:

- Educational qualifications
- Professional experience
- Relevant experience
- Other information

Requested by:	Authorized by:
GM	GM-HR
Date	Date

Form 12: Ethics and Conduct — Disclosure Format

Mark yes/no as per your awareness and understanding of issues related to ethics and conduct in the organization with which you are associated.

- Do you understand and support the company's code of ethics? Yes/No
- Are there any illegal, unethical or immoral practices or conduct anywhere within the company? Yes/No
- If the answer to the preceding question is "yes", list here, in full and complete details, all such practices or conduct. (Add annexure if necessary.)
- Are there any threats or promises been made to you in connection with your answers to the questions on this form? Yes/No
- If "yes" please identify them in full and complete details and notify the company management immediately.

I declare the information regarding the company's code of ethics and conduct is stated under no threats or obligation. The information provided by me is correct and true.

Signature Date

Designation

Department

Form 13: Training Schedule

S. No.	Basic need identified	No. of people
1.	(For example) Telephonic skills	
2.	Grooming	
3.		
4.		
5.		
6.		
7.		
8.		

Form 14: Training Feedback Form

Date:

Name:

Designation:

Training Programme:

Feedback about the training programme attended:

Q1. List what you learnt from this programme?

Q2. How this programme could have been more effective? Give suggestions.

Q3. Highlight the positive aspects of the programme?

Form 15: Management by Objective Appraisal Form

Date:

Name:

Designation:

Grade:

Department:

Date of Joining:

MBO Period: From to

Key Result Area 1.

Goals	Desired Results	Results Accomplished

Key Result Area 2.

Key Result Area 3.

Signature of the Appraisee:

Date:

Signature of the Appraiser:

Date:

Comments of the Appraiser

Form 16: Annual Appraisal Form

Name:

Designation:

Grade:

Department:

Date of Birth:

Date of Joining:

Period of Assessment: From to

A. To be completed by the appraisee

(Areas of personal growth)

(Training Attended)

B. Objectives Set	Tasks Accomplished

C. Performance Factors	Rating U 1	F 2	G 3	O 4
(Productivity)				
(Job knowledge)				
Column Total				
Multiply by Column Weight	×1	×2	×3	×4
Weighted Columnwise Total (WCT)				

Appraisal Index = Overall WCT/ Total no. of performance factors

Comments of the Appraisee:

Signature of the Appraiser:

Date:

Signature of the Appraisee:

Date:

Form 17: Increment Letter

Date:

Designation

Dear

Subject: Change in compensation and benefits

The management takes great pleasure in sharing with you about the change in emoluments for the current year which has been designed keeping in mind your excellent performance. Your good work has been recognized.

Your revised salary w.e.f. .... will be .... (CTC).

We wish you a great career!

Congratulations!

Yours sincerely,

Authorized by:

Name

Designation

Company Name

Form 18: Appreciation Letter

Hello Team,

Great job performance and good achievement of targets!!

I am pleased to see such great performance and am hopeful that similar performance shall continue and should pay off. Looking forward to such delivery month by month and a year's crores of turnover.

Regards,

Team Leader

Form 19: LEAVE FORMATS

Optional Leave Format — Annexure 1

Name of the Employee

Department

Application date	Leave date	Purpose/ Occasion	Sign	Approved by

Sick Leave Format — Annexure 2

Name of the employee:

Total sick leave entitlement:

Can avail till:

Application date	Leave dates From To	No. of days	Total leave taken	Purpose of absence	Location	Sign	Approved by	Admn. Dept.

Casual Leave Format — Annexure 3

Name of the employee:

Total casual leave entitlement:

Can avail till:

Application date	Leave dates From To	No. of days	Total leave taken	Purpose of absence	Location	Sign	Approved by	Admn. Dept.

Privilege Leave Format — Annexure 4

Name of the employee:

Total privilege leave entitlement:

Can avail till:

Application date	Leave dates From To	No. of days	Total leave taken	Purpose of absence	Location	Sign	Approved by	Admn. Dept.

Special Sick Leave Format — Annexure 5

Name of the employee:

Total special sick leave entitlement:

Can avail till:

Application date	Leave dates From To	No. of days	Total leave taken	Purpose of absence	Location	Sign	Approved by	Admn. Dept.

Form 20: Illness/Injury Form

XYX Ltd. requires a medical proof about the employee's/family member's illness, injury or death in the family which will be documented as reason for any absence from work. The medical practitioner needs to specify the length of treatment and expected recovery. Following is the format of the desired medical proof.

.... is under medical observation and unable to perform his/her job from ....to ....

I certify that the information provided by me is correct and therefore it will impair this person to perform his/ her job with XYX Ltd. due to his/her current medical condition.

Authorized by:

Signature of the doctor:

Date:

Signature of the employee:

Date:

Form 21: Experience Certificate

TO WHOMSOEVER IT MAY CONCERN

This is to certify that (Ms.XXXX) has served in our organization from (date-date) as a Design Engineer.

(Ms.XXXX) has resigned from the services of the organization of her own accord.

During her tenure with us we found her sincere and hard-working. It is also certified that she had drawn (Rs. ....../-pm) as her salary.

We wish her all success in her future endeavours.

GM Human Resources

Form 22: Exit Interview Form

Name:

Designation:

Grade:

Date of Joining:

Date of Termination:

Monthly Gross Salary:

Employee's Feedback:

Reason for Separation:

Future Contact Address:

Observations on:

1. Company rules
2. Co-workers
3.
4.

Form 23: Final Relieving Letter

Date:

Ms XXXX

Delhi – H.O.

Sub: Relieving Letter

Dear Mr. XXXX,

This has reference to your letter of resignation dated, wherein you have requested to be relieved from the services of the company at the earliest.

We inform you that your resignation is hereby accepted and you are being relieved from the services of the company with effect from....

We also certify that your full and final settlement of account has been cleared with the organization.

Your contributions to the organization and its success will always be appreciated. We at (ZZZZ India Pvt. Ltd.) wish you all the best in your future endeavours.

Yours sincerely,

For ZZZZ India Pvt. Ltd.

GM Human Resources

Section IV

Avenues and Scope

Where to do PG in HR/OB

This section has a list of the institutions which offer post-graduate degree in Human Resources and Organizational Behaviour. Another list in this section contains addresses of some websites which offer recruitment. The PG passouts can explore these websites for their dream jobs. The sites are also useful for the people who are already in a job but desire a change. Further, there is a list of various HR openings and their approximate corresponding remunerations.

Institutes Offering PG in HR/OB

1. MA Psychology
   Specialization: Organizational Behaviour
   Department of Psychology
   North Campus, Arts Faculty, University of Delhi,
   Delhi - 110007
   Ph: (011) 7667725 Ext.: 1313, 1314
   Main Campus Office: (011) 6882503, 6111955.
   Ext: 273 (South Campus)
   Fax: 91-11-7666285 (Main Campus)

2. PG in Personnel Management & Industrial Relations
   XLRI, Jamshedpur, Circuit House Area (East),
   Jamshedpur-831001
   Jharkhand. India
   Ph.: +91-657-398 3333
   Fax: +91-657-222 7814
   email: xlwebmaster@xlri.ac.in
   Admission Office : admis@xlri.ac.in
   Media Contact: exlink@xlri.ac.in

3. Master of Arts in Human Resource Management & Labour Relations
   TISS, Tata Institute of Social Sciences
   P. O. Box 8313, Deonar
   Mumbai, 400 088. India
   Ph.: 91-22-25525000 (Board Number)
   Fax: 25525050
   Website: www.tiss.edu
   email: webmaster@tiss.edu

4. MA in Human Resource and Organizational Development (MHROD)
   Department of Commerce
   Faculty of Commerce and Business,
   Delhi School of Economics, University of Delhi
   Delhi - 110007. India
   Tel: 766-7891, 766-6781, 766-7725. Extn.: 1630
   Fax: 766-6781
   Website: www.commdsedu.org

5. MA Organizational Behaviour
   Amity University
   Amity-Delhi/Noida Campus

Block - E2
Sector-125, Noida – 201303 (UP)
email: admissions@amity.edu

6. MHRM (Master of Human Resource Management)
Andhra University
Waltair, Visakhapatnam
Andhra Pradesh – 530003. India
Tel: +91-891-2844000
Fax: +91-891-2755324, 2525611
Website: www. andhrauniversity.info
Email: aulibra@md2.vsnl.net.in

7. M.Sc. Applied Psychology
Specialization: Organizational Behaviour
Barathiar University
Department of Psychology
Coimbatore – 641046
Tamil Nadu, India
Website: www.b-u.ac.in

8. MA in Human Resource Management
Jamia Millia Islamia, Jamia Nagar
Delhi – 110025. India
Website : jmi.nic.in

9. MA in Psychology
Specialization in Organizational Behaviour
Jamia Millia Islamia, Jamia Nagar
Delhi – 110025. India
Website : jmi.nic.in

10. MBA Human Resource Development
Jiwaji University,
Gwalior – 474 011, Madhya Pradesh. India
Tel: +91-751-341450/341 896, 341 095
Fax: +91-751-341 450
Website: Jiwaji.edu

11. MA in Psychology
University of Lucknow – IPPR Center
Uttar Pradesh – 226 007. India
Tel: +91-522-2741012-21, 2740467, 2740412
Fax: +91-522-2740467/2740412
Website: lkouniv.ac.in/lucknowuniv.org
email: vc@lkouniv.ac.in

12. MSc in Psychology
(Organizational Behaviour & Personnel Psychology)
Mysore University
Crawford Hall, Mysore – 570 005
Karnataka. India
Tel: +91-821-2419666/2419361
Fax: +91-821-2419363/2419301
Website: uni-mysore.ac.in
registrar@uni_mysore.ac.in/

13. MA Psychology
(Organizational Behaviour)
University of Mizoram
Tanhril, P.O. Box No. 190
Aizawl – 796 001, Mizoram. India
Tel: +91-389-2330652
Fax: +91-389-2330642
Website: mzu.edu.in
email: reg_mzu@yahoo.com

14. MSc Human Resource Development Psychology
University of Madras
University Centenary Building
Chepauk, Chennai – 600 005
Tamil Nadu. India
Tel: +91-044-2536 8778
Website: unom.ac.in
email: webmaster@unom.ac.in

15. MBA Human Resources
Manipal University
Madhav Nagar, Udupi – 576 104
Karnataka. India
Tel: +1800-425-6243 (for BSNL/MTNL subscribers)
+91-80-414-74392/93
Fax: +91-820-2571982
Website: manipal.edu/admissions.manipal.edu
email: reg.mahe@manipal.edu/
admissions@manipal.edu

16. MA Psychology
Master of Industrial Relations & Personnel Management
Nagpur University
Rabindra Nath Tagore Marg
Guru Nanak Bhawan
Nagpur – 440 001
Maharashtra, India

Tel: +91-712-523045/525417
Fax: +91-712-532841
Website: nagpuronline.com/academic/university.htm
email: vcnaguni@hotmail.com

17. MPM (Masters in Personnel Management)
University of Pune, Pune - 411 007
Maharashtra, India
Tel: +91-20-25696061/25690065/25693868//25601305
Fax: +91-20-25697388/25693899/25693233
Website: unipune.ernet.in
email: puvc@unipune.ernet.in/regis@unipune.ernet.in

18. Post Graduate Programme (PGP)
in Organizational Behaviour & HR Management
Indian Institute of Management, Kozhikode
IIMK Campus, P. O. Kozhikode
Kerala - 673 570, India
Tel: +91-495-2803001
Fax: +91-495-2803010-11
Website: www.iimk.ac.in

19. MBA
Specialization: Human Resource Management
Institute of Management
Nirma University, Sarkhej
Gandhinagar Highway, Chanlodia, via: Gota
Ahmedabad - 382 481, Gujarat, India
Tel: +91-2717-241900 to 04
Fax: +91-2717-241916
Webste: www.imnu.ac.in

20. MA/MSc Psychology
Specialization: Industrial & Organizational Behaviour
University of Rajasthan,
Jaipur, India
Website: www.uniraj.ernet.in

21. MBA (Human Resource)
Punjab University, University Business School
Arts Block III, Sector 14
Chandigarh – 160 014. Punjab. India
Tel: 0172-2541591
Website: puchd.ac.in
email: paubschair@pu.ac.in

22. MA Psychology
(Specialization:Organizational Behaviour & Management)
Sardar Patel Univeristy, Department of Psychology
Vallabh Vidyanagar – 388 120
Tel: 02692-226882 (O)
Fax: 02692-237258/236475
Website: www.spuvvn.edu
email: spu_psychology@yahoo.com

23. Master of Psychology
Specialization: Human Resource Development & Management, University of Allahabad
Senate Hall, Allahabad – 211 002
Uttar Pradesh. India
Tel: +91-532-2461157/1089
Fax: +91-532-2545021/2461083
Website: allduniv.ac.in
email: phrs@rediffmail.com/
registrarau@rediffmail.com

24. MHRDM
Jamnalal Bajaj Institute of Management Studies
Mumbai University
164, Backbay Reclamation, H. T. Parekh Marg
Road No. 3, Churchgate, Mumbai – 400 020
Maharashtra. India
Tel: +91-22-22024133/22024118/22025153
Fax: +91-22-22856905
Website: jbims.edu
email: director@jbims.edu

25. PGP–HR
Management Development Institute
Mehrauli Road, Sukhrali,
Gurgaon, Haryana – 122 007. India

Telefax: (91-124)2340147
Fax: 91-124-2341189
EPABX: (91-124) 4560800, 4013050-60, 2340153, 2340173, 2349831-36, Extn: 534, 537, 538
Liaison Office (Delhi): 011-26434674, 26438471
Website: www.mdi.ac.in
email: caomdp@mdi.ac.in

26. Post Graduate Diploma in Management (Human Resource)
Institute of Management Technology
Raj Nagar, Ghaziabad - 201 001, India
Tel: +91-0120-3002200
Fax: +91-0120-3002300
Website: www.imt.edu
email: info@imt.ac.in, info@imt.edu

27. MBA in HR
Bharathidasan Institute of Management
P. Box No. 12, MHD Complex
BHEL Campus, Tiruchirapalli - 620014
Tel: 0431-2520796, 2520502
Telefax: 0431-2520733
Website: www.bim.edu

28. PGP in Advanced Professional Competency
T. A. Pai Management Institute
Manipal - 576 104, Karnataka, India
Tel: 91-820-2571358, 2573162, 2573163, 2701000
Telefax: 91-820-2570699
Website: www.tapmi.org
email: director@mail.tapmi.org

29. PGDHR
Institute of Management Development and Research
DES Campus, Agarkar Road, Deccan Gymkhana
Pune - 411 004. India
Tel: 91-20-25653186, 91-20-25652754, 91-20-25657922
Fax: 91-20-25654371
Website: www.imdr.edu
email: registrar@imdr.edu

30. MHRM
Indian Institute of Social Welfare and Business Management, Management House
College Square West, Kolkata - 700 073. India

Tel: 91-33-22413648/3756/5792/8694
Fax: 91-33-22413975
Website: www.iiswbm.edu
email: iiswbm@iiswbm.edu

31. PGDM Specialization: HR
Welingkar Institute of Management Development & Research
L. Napoo Road, Near Matunga (Central Rly.)
Mumbai - 400 019. India
Tel: 91-22-24178300
Fax: 91-22-24105585
Website: welingkar.org

32. MBA
Specialization: Organization Management
Department of Management Studies, IIT, Delhi
Indian Institute of Technology,
Hauz Khas, New Delhi - 110 016. India
Tel: 011-26591171, Fax: 011-26862620
Website: www.iitdmba.com

33. Master's in Human Resource Development Management
K. J. Somaiya Institute of Management Studies & Research, Vidyanagar Vidyavihar (E)
Mumbai - 400 077. India
Tel: 91-022-67283000/67283050
Fax: 91-022-25157219
Website: simsr.somaiya.edu
email: info@simsir.somaiya.edu

34. PGDM, Specialization: Human Resource
Xavier Institute of Management & Entrepreneurship
Electronics City, Phase II
Hosur Road, Bangalore - 560 100, India
Tel: 91-80-28528477/28528597/28528598
Fax: 91-80-28528733 or 28520019
Website: http://www.xime.org
email: xime@xime.org

35. Master of Business Management
(Elective — Human Resource Management)
School of Management Studies
Cochin University of Science & Technology

Cochin - 682022. Kerala. India
Tel: 91 484 2575310, Extn : (247)/91 484 2550546
Fax : 0484 2575096
email : smsplacement2008@gmail.com

36. MBA Programme, Specialization: (dual) Human Resource
TKM Institute of Management
Musaliar Hills, Karuvelil P. O.
Kollam - 691505. Kerala. India
Ph: 0474 - 2482465, 2482466
Fax: 0474-2483527
Website: www.tkmim.org
email: tkmim@sancharnet.in

37. MBA, Specialization: HR & Behavioural Science
NMIMS University
School of Business Management
SVKM's NMIMS University
V.L. Mehta Road, Vile Parle (W)
Mumbai - 400 056. India
Tel: 91-22-2613 4577/2618 3688
Fax: 91-22-26114512
Website: www.nmims.edu
email: enquiry@nmims.edu

38. MBA, Specialization: OB & HRD
Faculty of Management Studies
North Campus
The Administrative Officer
University of Delhi, Delhi -110007
Tel: 91 -11-2766 6382/6387/6388

University of Delhi, South Campus
The Administrative Officer
Shanti Prasad Jain Advanced Management
Research Center
Benito Juarez Road, New Delhi -110021
Tel: 91 -11- 2687 5875/5879
Fax: 2687 - 5878
Website: www.fms.edu
email:admissions@fms.edu

39. PGDM-HR
International Management Institute
B -10, Qutab Institutional Area, Tara Crescent
New Delhi - 110016

Tel: 2696-1437/3519/6143, 2686-3701,
2652-8276/9237/9338/9239 extn: 3331.
(D) 2652-8277
Website: www.imi.edu
email: ratna ashokan@imi.edu

40. MBA, HRM
Symbiosis Institute of Management Studies
Opp. Station EME Workshop,
Range Hills Road, Khadki, Pune - 411020. India
Tel: (020) 30213201/239/250
Fax: (020) 30213333
Website: www.sims.edu
email: admissions @ sims.edu

41. MBA (HRM)
Badruka College PG Center
Department of Business Management
Kachiguda, Hyderabad - 500027, AP, India
Tel: 91-40-24658236,24606927
Website: www.badruka-mba.com
email: badruka@30gigs.com

42. MBA, Human Resources
BK School of Business Management
Gujarat University, Navrangpura
Ahmedabad - 380009, Gujarat. India
Tel: 91-7932407363, (M) 91-9327053930
Website: www.bkschool.in
email: info@bkschool.in

Popular Recruitment Sites

1. www.2myjobs.com
2. www.careerage.com
3. www.careerkhazana.com
4. www.clickjobs.com
5. www.coolavenues.com
6. www.indianjobsite.com
7. www.instantcareers.com
8. www.jobs20.com
9. www.jobsahead.com
10. www.jobsatanytime.com
11. www.jobsdb.com
12. www.jobsstreet.com
13. www.khojle.in
14. www.monster.com
15. www.naukri.com
16. www.placementindia.com
17. www.resumesindia.com
18. www.shine.com
19. www.timesjob.com
20. www.walkincareers.com
21. www.yellojobs.com

HR Positions and Remunerations

Designation	*Pay Scale*
• RECRUITMENT EXECUTIVE	7,500—12,000
• CONSULTANT	8,000—10,000
• COUNSELLOR	8,000—10,000
• HR EXECUTIVE (Generalizer)	8,000—12,000
• PROJECT LEADER	12,500—18,000

- RESOURCE EXECUTIVE (Based on backend job of recruitment) 8,000
- LECTURER 13,500—40,000
- HR MANAGER 50,000—1,00,000
- TRAINING MANAGER 21,000—30,000

(The pay scales quoted above are based on the general market trend. These can go higher as per the placement opportunities offered by the institutes teaching PG in courses in Human Resources or Organizational Behaviour or during the process of negotiation.)

❑

Index